The Penny Whistle™
CHRISTMAS
PARTY BOOK

INCLUDING
HANUKKAH,
NEW YEAR'S &
TWELFTH NIGHT
FAMILY PARTIES

By Meredith Brokaw & Annie Gilbar
DESIGNED & ILLUSTRATED BY JILL WEBER

A FIRESIDE BOOK PUBLISHED BY SIMON & SCHUSTER NEW YORK, LONDON, TORONTO, SYDNEY, TOKYO, SINGAPORE

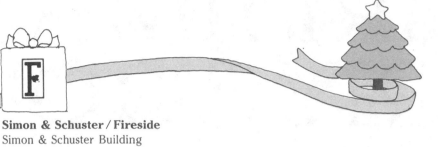

Simon & Schuster / Fireside
Simon & Schuster Building
Rockefeller Center
1230 Avenue of the Americas
New York, New York 10020

Text Copyright © 1991 by Meredith Brokaw and Annie Gilbar
Design and illustrations copyright © 1991 by Jill Weber

SIMON & SCHUSTER / FIRESIDE and colophon are registered trademarks of Simon & Schuster Inc.

Designed by Jill Weber
Manufactured in the United States of America

10 9 8 7 6 5 4 3 2 1

10 9 8 7 6 5 4 3 2 1 Pbk.

Library of Congress Cataloging in Publication Data

Brokaw, Meredith.
    The Penny Whistle Christmas party book: including Hanukkah, New Year's & Twelfth Night family parties / by Meredith Brokaw & Annie Gilbar; designed & illustrated by Jill Weber.
        p. cm.
    "A Fireside book"
    Includes index.
    Summary: Presents instructions on how to plan parties to celebrate Christmas, Hanukkah, and the New Year.
    1. Children's parties—Juvenile literature. 2. Christmas—Juvenile literature. 3. Hanukkah—Juvenile literature. 4. Entertaining—Juvenile literature. [1. Parties. 2. Christmas. 3. Hanukkah. 4. New Year.] I. Gilbar, Annie. II. Weber, Jill, ill. III. Title.
    GV1205.B66 1991
    793.2'1—dc20   91-18678
                                                                                           CIP
                                                                                           AC

ISBN 0-671-73794-5 Pbk.
        0-671-74797-5

DEDICATION

To our Families,
Always our Inspiration

ACKNOWLEDGMENTS

To all our friends, old and new, who generously shared their memories and ideas, so they can be retold and recycled for the pleasure of future generations. We thank you all!

Di Anderson
Bess and Louise Armstrong
Esther Ancoli-Barbasch
Pamela Belknap
Ann Connell Bergin
Joan and Pearl Borinstein
Betty Brown
Ronny Buns
Janet Carney
Jerry della Femina
Karen Emmer
Paula Englund
Nora Ephron
Don Ernstein
Sandy Fergusson
Luke Fieldler
Erin Fischer
Mark Friedland
Lois Gatchell
Miriam and Avigail Glazer
Edythe Harvey
Guy Harvey
Ruth Hirschhorn
Adrienne Horwitch

David, Sarah and Sonia Israel
Melanie Kirschner
Judy Licht
Herb Long
Elizabeth Mackey
Sydny Miner
Donald Nathanson
Sue O'Halloran
Betsy Radin
Jane Rascoff
Angela Rich
Kathy Robbins
Susan Russell
Heather Schieffert
Jed Schwartz
Wesley Schwartz
Joey, Obie and Donna Slamon
Mary Slawson
Martha Stewart
Bea and Janet Surmi
Jenna Trabulus
Ellen Wright
Barbara, Zev, Mina and David Yaroslavsky

CONTENTS

The Merriest Time of the Year

*'Twas the night before Christmas when all through the house
Not a creature was stirring . . .*

—Clement C. Moore, *The Night Before Christmas*
(New York: Golden Press, 1969)

Wait a minute! "Not a creature was stirring . . ."? Not in any house we know! As a matter of fact, in most homes, the "creatures" (better known as children) start "stirring" for the holidays just around the time they finish their Thanksgiving turkey, and every year, the anticipation continues to build until they are ready to burst by the time the holidays arrive.

Planning parties, decorating the house, making and wrapping presents, keeping secrets—'tis definitely "the season to be jolly," but also the season of great anticipation and intoxicating expectation, of happiness and joy, of warmth and togetherness, of sharing and giving.

❄

Erin Fischer reminds us that little kids like big projects. So try printing large images on wrapping paper or making a life-size Santa (see Deck the Halls).

❄

Try reading these wonderful Christmas stories to the children gathered at one of the parties: *A Christmas Carol* by Charles Dickens and *A Visit from Saint Nicholas*, the poem "The Night before Christmas" by Clement C. Moore.

How did it all start, this reveling that exalts Christmas trees, stockings on the mantel and wreaths on the doors, gift giving, and sweet feasts featuring cookies and gingerbread houses and candy canes?

From the earliest Christmas, and for centuries after, Christmas was the religious holiday that celebrated the birth of Christ. The word Christmas comes from the Old English *Cristes mæsse*, which means Christ's mass. The holiday is traditionally celebrated on December 25.

Many countries have celebrated the Christmas season, and traditions from one nation have traveled to others. In was in Germany that Saint Nicholas was born, later becoming Santa Claus in the United States. It was in Germany, also, that the first Christmas trees, adorned with apples, appeared.

In England, the custom of sending Christmas cards began; it was the English who first hung mistletoe in the doorways, and English children hung up stockings for Father Christmas. It was also the English who served goose for dinner and plum pudding for dessert, and they began the custom of singing religious hymns (composed mostly around the 1800s) while strolling around the neighborhood. In Ireland, children put lighted candles in the windows so outsiders would feel welcome. In France, children still leave their shoes in front of the fireplace for *Père Noël* to fill with gifts. The French and the Spaniards are famous for their Nativity scenes that are displayed in every village. In Mexico, people celebrate during the nine days before Christmas, called *las posadas*, and on Christmas Day, the children get to break *piñatas*, which drop gifts for everyone. Today, in nearly every country, Saint Nicholas, Santa Claus, or any of his many assistants, brings gifts to children everywhere.

Even though Christmas is still celebrated as a religious holiday, it has become, in the last centuries, more of a secular celebration marking a festive holiday season. And whether it's Christmas festivities, Hanukkah celebrations, or social gatherings to rejoice in the hopes for the New Year, 'tis truly the season for families to celebrate together. Sharing the experiences of the holidays with friends and family, particularly when children are included, is what memories are made of. Making ornaments and decorating the tree, caroling, wrapping gifts, constructing menorahs, building a village made of candy houses, creating a breakfast for Mom and Dad on New Year's Day—these are all activities for *everyone* to share.

And that's the key. The *Penny Whistle Christmas Party Book* is full of parties designed for children and parents to celebrate *together*. You'll find Santa's Workshop, where the children make gifts for their families and friends while their parents get a day off for their own holiday shopping; a Tree-Trimming Party, where the adults and the children decorate their own trees with ornaments they have made together; a "White Christmas" party, where *everything* is white (this is especially appropriate for those who never see snow at Christmas); a holiday village party, where the children build an entire town (including a variety of candy houses and a sugar cube church); a family reunion, with children creating a "family tree"; two Hanukkah parties, where the children make their own menorahs and edible dreidels; a New Year's Day brunch, where the children cook for their parents; and finally a Twelfth Night celebration, a joyous farewell to the holiday season.

And there's more: thoughts on giving parties; instructions on making over thirty ornaments and decorations, including a mammoth Santa, walnut and stocking Advent calendars, clusters of angels, Christmas stockings and Gingerbread Men, unusual gift wrappings; words to some popular Christmas and Hanukkah songs; and over seventy-five different games, puzzles, and activities to play during the parties and throughout the holiday season.

So, as you leaf through these pages and plan your parties to celebrate this holiday season, we wish you peace, joy, Merry Christmas, Happy Hanukkah, and a very Happy New Year!

❆ In some northern European countries, families burn Yule Logs, which are believed to have magic powers.

MERRY CHRISTMAS IN DIFFERENT COUNTRIES

CHINA
Sheng Dan Kuai Le

DENMARK
Glaedelig Jul

FINLAND
Hauskaa Joulua

FRANCE
Joyeux Nöel

GERMANY / AUSTRIA
Fröhliche Weihnachten

GREECE
Kala Christougenna

HUNGARY
Kellemes Karácsonyi Ünnepeket

ITALY
Buon Natale

JAPAN
Meri Kurisumasu

THE NETHERLANDS
Zalig Kerstfeest

NORWAY
Gledelig Jul

POLAND
Wesolych Swiat

PORTUGAL / BRAZIL
Boas Festas

RUSSIA
S Rozhdestvom Kristovym

SPAIN / MEXICO
Feliz Navidad

SWEDEN
God Jul

❆ Don't feel sorry for babies born on Christmas Day, says Meredith, who is one of them. When she was young, she was happy to celebrate her birthday on Christmas because she figured all the fuss and excitement was for her birthday. Now, as the years go by, she figures it's great to have her birthday get lost among the festivities.

Deck the Halls

The excitement level of a child's Christmas usually begins to rise long before December 25. Such heightened anticipation produces children who are eagerly searching for ways to become involved in the process of the Christmas season. Having a preholiday party to create Christmas ornaments and decorations guarantees that everyone will get into the spirit of the season, and will involve your children by channeling their imaginative and enterprising energies into making some wonderful creations.

The following pages illustrate things you and your child can make together *before* the holiday fever really hits. Other less-involved and less-elaborate decorations are listed within each party as party activities.

WALNUT ADVENT CALENDAR

Advent is the name given to the season that begins four Sundays before Christmas. It reminds everyone that Christmas is on its way, and that the time has come to prepare for the holiday. Many families use a special Advent calendar to count down the days before December 25, beginning on the first day of December. To children, Advent calendars are intriguing, for each date in the month of December preceding Christmas holds a secret. The dates on an Advent calendar are covered, and only with the arrival of each day is its number exposed when that window is opened, revealing a picture or object that has historically had religious significance.

Many traditional versions of the Advent calendar are available through catalogs or wherever Christmas cards are sold. You can also make an Advent calendar, though if you make it with your child, the surprises behind the windows will no longer be surprises! This version, inspired by Erin Fischer, an artist from Prosser, Washington, is not a traditional Advent calendar, since it counts only the twelve days before Christmas and uses novelty items. But it is simple and fun for children to make, even for the little ones.

You can make the calendar as elaborate or as modest as you like. You will need:

1 empty egg carton (cardboard or Styrofoam)

Spray paint for the egg carton

12 walnuts (open carefully with a table knife and use the meats for something else)

Tempera paints for the walnut shells

12 miniature surprises (coins, toys, candy, messages)

Felt-tip markers

❄ For an added treat, you can include messages in each walnut.

Spray the egg carton with any color paint you like. Let dry. You can glue anything decorative to the outside: pictures from old Christmas cards, beads, sequins, yarn, or family memorabilia.

Clean out the walnut halves and paint the outside of each half. Let dry. Now insert a surprise into twelve of the halves and cover each with the corresponding half. Place each complete walnut in a pocket of the egg carton. When dry, number the top of each walnut, one through twelve, using paint or felt-tip markers.

That's it. Display the Walnut Advent Calendar in a prominent place in the house. On the twelfth day before Christmas, your child opens walnut number twelve; on the eleventh day, walnut number eleven; and so on. It's a countdown until Christmas!

❄ Decorate the walnuts with paint, ribbons, or sequins, or decorate any way your child likes.

❄
Last year, Jenna Trabulus's Christmas stocking was a Red Riding Hood boot trimmed with red and white polka-dotted fabric.

❄
In Big Timber, Montana, Heather Schieffert's dog Rebel always has his own Christmas stocking, which Heather fills with Milk-Bones.

CHRISTMAS STOCKING

There are as many variations of the Christmas Stocking as there are of the story of who started the custom of hanging Christmas stockings. One favorite tale tells of a smart-alecky Dutch boy who, tired of the "ordinary" custom of leaving wooden shoes outside the door for Saint Nick to fill with goodies, decided instead to leave a stretchable stocking, figuring he would receive more candy that way. No one knows if Saint Nick fell for the trick and left extra treats for this clever chap, but they do say that the other children caught on, and thereafter many Dutch children took to hanging Christmas stockings on their doors.

Christmas stockings come in all shapes and sizes. You can buy them ready-made almost anywhere during the holidays. We've seen fireplace mantels covered with stockings made out of decorated felt, denim (one friend's version, a cowboy boot, had a child's leather cowboy belt sewn across the top), fake fur, and even one made out of fuzzy yarn and shaped like a baby's bootee for a newborn's first Christmas.

The best part about making family Christmas stockings is the tradition of using them year after year. Some families choose to make new stockings every year, embroidering the date on each so they have memories of every Christmas. Other families make one when a child is young and add different decorations every year as the child grows older.

The following description is of one of the stockings that Edythe Harvey, Meredith's grandmother, made over forty years ago, and which has been hung by the fireplace with care every year since. This is a simple yet decorative stocking that can be made with your children and used each Christmas.

Cut a stocking out of two pieces of felt—14 to 16 inches long by about 8 inches wide at the bottom is a nice size. We make ours red on one side and green on the other. Cutting the fabric with pinking shears makes a neat and even outline that doesn't need hemming. You can individualize the stocking by sewing or gluing cutout felt shapes (such as ballet slippers, soccer balls, dolls, trees, skateboards, animals, or cars) to one side of the stocking to represent the owner's interests. You can also add beads, sequins, or embroidery. Use glitter pens or embroidery to personalize each stocking. (Note: The glitter must dry overnight.)

Now make a border with a contrasting color of felt and sew or glue it across the top. Sew or glue a handle out of felt or ribbon at one end of the border. You'll be glad on future Christmases if you remember to sew or write the date on one side of the stocking! Now sew the front and back together, leaving the top open for the upcoming deposit of goodies.

This can become an heirloom that your children will treasure as adults. Don't let another year go by without this special tradition!

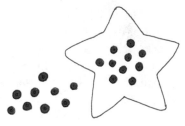

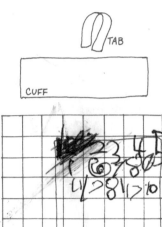

TAB

CUFF

✳ Another variation of the Christmas Stocking is to glue tiny toys and "packages" (tiny matchboxes wrapped to look like gifts) *on* the stocking as decoration.

✳ Use baby socks to make miniature Christmas stockings and fill with miniature toys and candies. Great as party favors or to give out to younger children.

❄

Kids' stocking stuffers: Anything small—toys, chocolate kisses, plastic animals, jelly beans, pennies, flip books, instruments, kazoos, crystal rocks, magnets, cars and trucks, miniature dolls, erasers.

❄

The bigger the stocking, the easier it will be to make and fill it.

❄

Donald Nathanson made a stocking trimmed in cartoons he had cut out, covered in clear contact paper and stapled to the fabric.

ADVENT CHRISTMAS STOCKINGS

Neither an ordinary stocking nor an ordinary Advent calendar, here is a twofer that can be used to mark the days before Christmas and then used again for Santa's visit on Christmas morning. Just follow the general directions for the felt Christmas Stocking (page 14). Once the stocking is cut out, place it flat on the table. Cut out 2-inch-square pieces of felt in bright colors—they can be bigger, but you must be able to fit twelve of these on the Christmas Stocking shape. Glue or stitch each square to the front of the stocking, leaving the top end open (it's much easier for young children to glue these on, while older children can easily stitch them). Number each pocket, from one through twelve, with glitter glue. You can also add the family name, and any other message.

When the design is finished, remove the stocking to an out-of-the-way place to let the numbers dry overnight. The next day, fill each pocket with tiny gifts (rubber stamps, toys, penny candies, coins, stickers, or jewelry).

You are now ready to present your child with his Advent Christmas Stocking. The process is the same as for the Walnut Advent Calendar (page 13). Starting twelve days before Christmas, allow your child to open one pocket a day beginning with pocket number twelve.

RICE KRISPIES™ CHRISTMAS TREES

These mini trees are delightful centerpieces for any Christmas table. You can also use them in the "Build a Village" party. Make them the day before any party you are giving.

¼ cup margarine
One 10-ounce package (about 40) large marshmallows or 4 cups miniature marshmallows
Green food coloring
6 cups Rice Krispies™ cereal
1 cup Red Hots™ candy

In a large saucepan, melt the margarine over low heat. Add the marshmallows and stir until they are completely melted. Add 10 drops of green food coloring. Remove from the heat.

Add the cereal to the marshamallow mixture. Stir with a wooden spoon until the cereal is well covered by the marshmallows. Add 10 more drops of green food coloring to give an uneven shade to the mixture.

Lightly oil or butter a 1-cup funnel. Pack it full with the cereal-marshmallow mixture (insert the funnel into a mug to hold it steady while you work). Mold mixture with a wooden spoon or with wet fingers. When you are done with one tree, turn it upside down and unmold it on a plate or wax paper. While still warm, press the Red Hots™ randomly into the tree to look like ornaments. If you want to decorate it with different kinds of candies, use Royal Icing™ (page 19) for glue. When the tree is done, place on a platter or put into a small clay pot filled with crushed aluminum foil to give the tree an appropriate base. Place in the center of your holiday table.

NOTE: The 1-cup funnel will make five trees. You can vary the funnel size and make larger or smaller trees.

MAKING PAINT NAMES

Thanks to the invention of "puffy paint" and glitter glue, children's names can be written, dried, and then used as place cards, as decorations, and for games (see page 76 in the "Family Holiday Reunion" party). Remember, they need to dry overnight, but you can also make them a week before you need them.

Using squeeze bottles of "puffy paint" or glitter glue, write the names in script letters about 1½ inches high on wax paper. Let them dry. The next day, the names will simply lift off the paper.

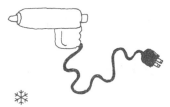

❄ Buy a mini glue gun. It will be useful in every facet of the holiday preparations, from making ornaments to gift wrapping to making stockings and wreaths, and is available in most drugstores, stationery stores, and hardware stores. Small ones cost about five dollars (and come with four glue sticks).

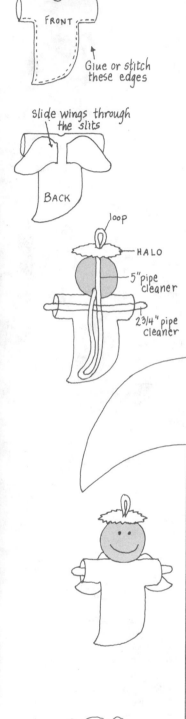

ANGELS IN CLUSTERS

What's better than one glorious Christmas angel? A dozen or more, of course. These angels can hang alone or in clusters, as guardians in your children's rooms, in any corner of the house, or from the center of a canopy at the "I'm Dreaming of a White Christmas" party. They also make lovely Christmas tree ornaments and/or party favors. To make three dozen angels you will need:

Four 12-by-12-inch squares of felt, multicolored or all white
Elmer's glue™
A permanent black fine-line marker
36 ¾-inch wooden beads
36 chenille pipe cleaners, multicolored or white
Fishing line
A tree branch or twigs tied together with raffia (optional)
White Christmas-tree lights (optional)

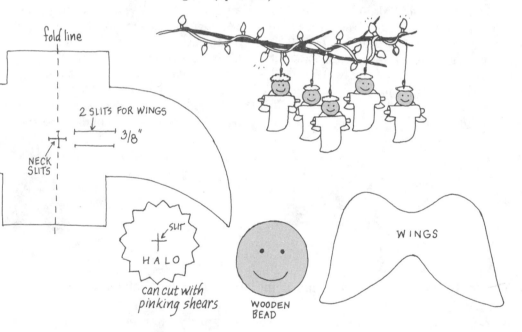

Transfer the pattern above to a piece of felt. You will be able to get nine angels out of each piece. Cut out the pieces. Cut a cross in the center of the halo. Cut two ⅜-inch slits on the gown as shown in the drawing. Glue or stitch the edges together, leaving openings in the sleeves. Slip the wings through the slits in the gown. Using black marker, draw a face on the bead. Cut the pipe cleaner into a 5-inch length and a 2¾-inch length. Thread the longer piece of pipe cleaner through the halo, bead, and gown, and make a loop at the top. Thread the shorter length of pipe cleaner through the sleeves, curving it gently upward at the ends. Tie a piece of fishing line through the loop. If you're hanging a number of angels together, vary the length of the fishing line so some hang lower and some higher. You can hang them from a branch, or from twigs that have been tied together with raffia, and then string Christmas lights in and around the branch.

❋ Since you can roll and reroll gingerbread cookie dough only so many times, use the scraps for free-form sculptures.

GINGERBREAD MEN

Delicious and adorable, Gingerbread Men have become a Christmas tradition all over the country. This recipe from *Martha Stewart's Christmas Entertaining** (New York: Crown, 1989) is absolutely delectable, easy to make (especially when you do it with your children), and truly foolproof. One Christmas, when celebrating the holiday away from home, the Brokaws were caught with a bare Christmas tree in the living room because ornaments mailed from home didn't arrive. Meredith baked up a batch of Gingerbread Men and voilà—a decorated tree!

To add variety to the group, you can ice them in different colors or, before baking, bend the arms and/or legs in funny positions. You can also personalize your Gingerbread Men; cookies with names written in icing can be used as place cards, given out as presents, or hung on the tree.

This recipe makes three- to four-dozen Gingerbread Men, depending on the size of your cookie cutter.

GINGERBREAD DOUGH
1 cup dark molasses
½ cup light brown sugar
½ cup granulated sugar
4 teaspoons ground ginger
4 teaspoons ground cinnamon
¾ tablespoon baking soda
1 cup (2 sticks) unsalted butter,
    at room temperature
2 large eggs, lightly beaten
6 cups sifted all-purpose flour

ROYAL ICING™
1 cup sifted confectioner's sugar
1 large egg white
Food coloring

Place the molasses, sugar, ginger, and cinnamon in a double boiler over medium heat. When the sugar has melted, add the baking soda and stir. When the mixture bubbles up, remove from the heat.

Place the butter in a large mixing bowl. Add the hot molasses mixture and stir well. Let the mixture cool to about 90°F and then add the eggs. Gradually add the flour, 1 cup at a time, while beating. (This is best done with an electric mixer, but you can use a wooden spoon.)

Preheat the oven to 325°F and line thick baking sheets with parchment paper.

Shape the dough into a neat rectangle, place on a well-floured board, and roll out until ¼ inch thick. Cut into shapes (gingerbread men), place shapes on the baking sheets, and bake for 15 to 20 minutes or until firm to the touch. Let cool on racks.

Mix the powdered sugar and egg white. Divide the mixture among the small bowls and tint each a different color with a few drops of food coloring. (Author's Note: Test it yourself—fewer drops make a lighter frosting; more drops make it darker. Be careful: You can't make too dark icing lighter.) Spread or pipe onto the cooled cookies and let set.

Meredith's advice: If you expect to use these as tree ornaments, make a small hole at the top of each with a toothpick before you bake the cookies. Then, when the cookies are still warm, enlarge the holes a bit (they sometimes close up after they are baked), so you can easily thread ribbon through. Since the children will be decorating these cookies, you'll need a lot of frosting and bowls of candies—M&M's™, gumdrops, dragées, sprinkles, colored sugar—any tiny candies your child loves.

Note: You can bake these on a greased cookie sheet instead of using parchment.

MAKES 3 TO 4 DOZEN
* used by permission of the author

Bess Armstrong and her son Luke Fiedler, 3, make 200 Gingerbread Men every year for their annual decorating party. They collect plastic margarine containers and fill them with different colored frostings and the many types of candies guests use for decorating the Gingerbread Men.

❄️
After Christmas, Wesley Schwartz put his Gingerbread Log Cabin high up in the tree outside his bedroom window so the birds could enjoy what he and his brothers couldn't finish eating.

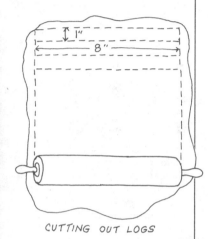

CUTTING OUT LOGS

GINGERBREAD LOG CABIN

This delightful old-fashioned log cabin is truly easy for parents and children to make. It doesn't matter if you have never baked a gingerbread house before—this log cabin is uncomplicated, fun to bake and to put together. When it's done, use it in your "Build a Village" party.

1. Start by making the Gingerbread Dough (page 19) and the House Mortar (page 66) and collecting some decorating candy (use the same kinds as we use in making the Candy House, page 66).

2. Cover a stiff piece of cardboard (about 24 inches square) with white freezer paper. This is the base for the house.

3. Roll out the Gingerbread Dough to about ¼ inch. With a knife, cut out the following:

> LOGS: Twenty-eight 8 by 1 inch (for the 4 walls), two 5 by 1 inch, two 4 by 1 inch, and two 2 by 1 inch; also cut out 14 spacers (little pieces of gingerbread about ½ inch square).
> WINDOWS: 1½ by 1½ inches (4 will look great)
> DOORS: 1½ by 3 inches
> CHIMNEY: use cookies or marshmallows
> ROOF: 2 pieces, each 4 by 6 inches

4. Bake these, one sheet at a time, leaving space between the logs. Be sure to bake them long enough so the dough is firm.

5. Assemble the log cabin by putting the icing on the ends of each log and assembling as you would with Lincoln logs™ until you get to the peak. (See instructions with drawing.)

6. Ice the roof and base (the cardboard). Attach the roof to the house with the icing. Sprinkle the whole thing with shredded coconut.

7. Decorate the windows and doors first, then attach them to the house.

8. Decorate the house with candies, using the House Mortar as glue.

WINDOW   DOOR

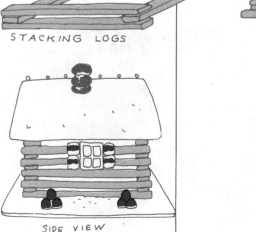

STACKING LOGS

SIDE VIEW

FRONT

STAINED GLASS WINDOWS

Turning your ordinary glass panes into magical Stained Glass Windows for the holidays is an easy task and fun for children of all ages.

For Christmas, you can create "cathedral" windows. Trace or photocopy these drawings and enlarge them at your local copier store and use them as patterns. (Other patterns can be found in children's coloring books. Or draw an angel, a tree, carolers, or let your child come up with his own ideas.) Tape the drawing facing in on the outside of the window. Using acrylic paints, simply follow the outlines on the inside of the window with black paint (this makes the windows look like they are "leaded" glass) and then fill in the shapes with paint. (Younger children may appreciate masking tape to help outline the images and to keep the paint from running over the borders of the design.)

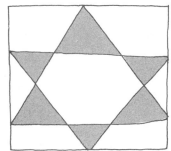

For Hanukkah, images of menorahs, lit candles, dreidels, *gelt* (money), or any winter scenes are appropriate. Using the blue and white colors of Hanukkah will make beautiful windows that will glow at night.

MAMMOTH SANTA

Make a larger-than-life Santa with your child to hang in his room, on his door, or in a prominent spot for the whole family to enjoy. He can be a traditional Santa or, with some imagination, a funny, more original one.

Our Santa, about 4 to 5 feet high, is made out of cardboard shapes. You cut out a square for the body, ovals for the arms and legs, and a circle for the face. Attach them to each other with glue or with metal fasteners (which will enable your child to move the arms and legs). You can cover the individual pieces of cardboard with Christmas wrapping. Shiny red, green, white, or patterned paper will give Santa's costume a whimsical holiday air. When the pieces are put together, glue on cotton for a large beard, and draw in the eyes, smiling mouth, and rosy cheeks.

To make Santa three-dimensional, you can put a real belt across his middle, real boots on his feet, a real cap on his head, and real mittens on his hands.

FANTASY WREATHS

Christmas wreaths, hung on front doors all over the world, signal to neighbors and friends that the season has arrived. Most traditional wreaths are made out of evergreen and other branches, and are sometimes adorned with fruits and holly. But for children, fantasy wreaths, made out of unusual combinations of decorations, are more fun to design and make, and bring smiles to all who view them.

You can make any or all of the following wreaths a couple of weeks before the holidays. You might want to let your child choose where to hang his wreath (he may select to hang one on the door to his own room, in the doorway of the "party" room, or on that old front door).

Pretzel Wreath

Combining the holiday wreath with a favorite kid's food—pretzels—results in an imaginative and definitely novel decoration that our friend Paula Englund has been making with her children for over twenty years. You will need:

> 11 large hard pretzels
> A glue gun or white glue
> 2 yards of red satin ribbon, 1 inch wide
> Cranberries
> Soft florist wire or an ornament hanger

On a flat cutting board, place six pretzels in a circle. In between and on top of each of those, lay the other five pretzels (see drawing). Using your glue gun, glue the top pretzels to the bottom ones wherever they touch. Let dry for about 5 minutes. Now weave red ribbon through the pretzel holes starting from whatever you chose to be the top (leave a little piece to tie a bow). Glue cranberries to the wreath. Let dry. To hang, tie some florist wire at the top or use an ornament hanger.

❄ Buy a simple small wreath and give it to your child to decorate as he wishes.

❄ When Meredith opened her first Penny Whistle Toys Store in 1978, she and her partner, Mary Slawson, tied 4-inch metal whistles to each package as a store promotion. With the leftover whistles, Mary invited friends and their children to a tree-trimming party and asked her guests to tie red ribbons on the whistles and hang them on her tree. The whistles, needless to say, were a great hit with everyone, especially the kids!

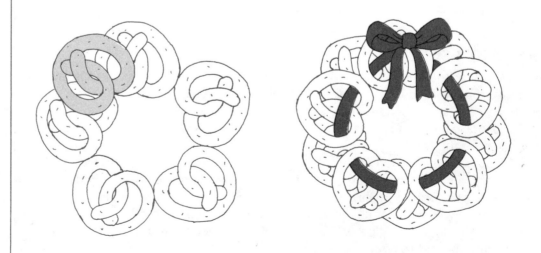

Ribbon Wreath

Here's what you do with all those curly ribbons you have collected during the preparation for the holidays: Make them into a Ribbon Wreath! Cut a wreath shape out of hard cardboard. Take 4- to 6-inch-lengths of ribbon and make them curl using the blade of a scissor (be sure to do this yourself if your children are very young). Glue one end of each ribbon curl to the base of the wreath, making sure to glue them very close together. When the wreath is covered with ribbons, start again, gluing a second pile of ribbons on top of and between the others, until your wreath looks like this. You can use ribbons in all colors, or just red and green, or all gold, or all pastels—whatever your child loves.

Gift Wreath

What could be a more delightful wreath than one made out of presents and toys? You will need:

> A glue gun or white glue
> Assorted miniature toys and wrapped gifts, or homemade ornaments
> A cutout of a wreath-shaped circle, 3 inches wide, in hard cardboard
> Lots of mini bows and ribbons in all colors and widths

Glue the miniature toys and wrapped gifts (see page 15 for instructions on making mini gifts), or some homemade ornaments (see page 44), to the wreath. Place them randomly, wherever you like. In between the toys and gifts, glue the bows and ribbons. Once you have one layer of toys and gifts glued on to the cardboard wreath, start again, piling the toys and gifts all askew one on the other (see drawing). The result is a virtual treasure chest of toys to enchant even Santa!

✳
Give Christmas cookies as gifts. Have your child pack three cookies he made in a basket that he has decorated. Wrap in colored cellophane, tie with a ribbon, and fasten with a card that your child has made.

✳
You can spray-paint the whole wreath a single color.

Gift Wrapping & Card Making

GIFT WRAPPING

Involve your children in wrapping every gift they are giving this season. When the process of wrapping gifts is entertaining, challenging, and creative, and when a child spends time wrapping a gift himself, gift giving becomes as much fun as gift getting. Show them that even the smallest, most inexpensive gift is enhanced by thoughtful gift wrapping. Remind them that the anticipation of the gift starts with the wrapping and that by designing their wrappings, they are giving a part of themselves to their friends and relatives.

Encourage kids to substitute creativity for dollars and create wrappings that fit the people who will open them. *Personalization* is the key to successful gift wrapping. Does Grandma love to cook? Wrap her gift in butcher paper stamped with outlines of cooking utensils; send a new recipe as a card; glue miniature toy food to the top of the gift box. Does your best friend love football? Wrap his gift in the sports page of the newspaper; turn football tickets into cards; glue a mini football to the box.

Inspire kids to make their wrapped creations their art and to use drawings they have made in their wrapping. Remind them that by giving their art, they are really giving two gifts to their friends; the art they have created on the outside will complement the gift on the inside! Handmade wrapping teaches children that the fact they did something themselves can mean even more to the receiver than the gift inside. And, in fact, each gift-wrapped creation is a work of art in itself, a gift that will be prized by the friend who will open it.

The suggestions for making cards and gift wrappings are illustrated on pages 26–30. Each is simple and can be made by children of all ages.

CARDS

Sir Henry Cole, a founder of the Victoria and Albert Museum in London, gets credit for starting the tradition of sending Christmas cards in the mid-1800s. It seems that one Christmas, the busy Mr. Cole found that he had no time to write his traditional Christmas letters to his family and friends; so he commissioned an artist, John Horsely, to create a decorated card that was printed with an apology for not writing a personal note and sent it to everyone on his list. By the next year, the practice had caught on and a British company, Charles Goodall and Sons, issued the first Christmas cards that were sold to the public. Once the King and Queen took to including Christmas cards with their gifts, a new tradition was born.

A gift card can be both the finishing touch to a wrapped gift and a message bringing good wishes for the holidays. While store-bought cards can also be personalized with written massages and drawings, it is the handmade card that is most memorable.

❄ In your local craft or hobby shop, buy wooden letters to spell a name, "stuff," or other words; paint them, and glue them on a box for a special gift.

❄ For the child who lives for trains, buy a tiny plastic train and glue it on his gift.

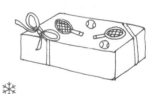

❄ Pearl Borinstein creates dioramas on wrapped gifts by gluing on miniature figures and toys with a glue gun. For her daughter's tennis teacher, she created a tennis scene with tiny balls and rackets arranged on top, and glued tiny plastic dogs on a gift to a friend who loves dogs.

❄ Use a photo of the giver as the gift card. Glue onto a paper card and have the giver write his name. Or if you have the recipient's picture, use that on the gift card.

CARDS

WE WISH YOU
A MERRY CHRISTMAS
WE WISH YOU A
MERRY CHRISTMAS
JOY TO THE WORLD

Every invitation in this book can also be a holiday card; just substitute your greetings for the invitation copy.

Don't forget Victorian designs, paper doilies, buttons, lace ribbons, swatches of fabric, or even potpourri can be glued onto a card for a romantic masterpiece.

Cut out the star using silver paper. Make three slits and weave in three gold, red, or blue strips. You can write the message on these strips or on the back.

JOY

Cut out two paper stocking shapes and glue together. Write the message on a slip of paper and stick inside.

M·E·R·R·Y
M·E·R·R·Y· CHRISTMAS

SEASON'S GREETINGS

FOLD

Cut out snowflakes and paste on shiny paper.

ADD A STAR TO MAKE A TREE

MERRY CHRISTMAS MERRY CHRISTMAS MERRY CHRISTMAS MERRY

Even young children can cut out a spiral shape. Make it about ¾ inch wide and have them write their message up and down the spiral.

JOY TO THE WORLD
to Charlie, Clove, Molly, James & Julie

Any of the paper chains we have included in the ornament section (see page 45) can be used as cards.

Save your child's drawings throughout the year and let him use them for holiday cards.

Have your child glue a photo of his face on a drawing he did or on a funny cutout from a magazine.

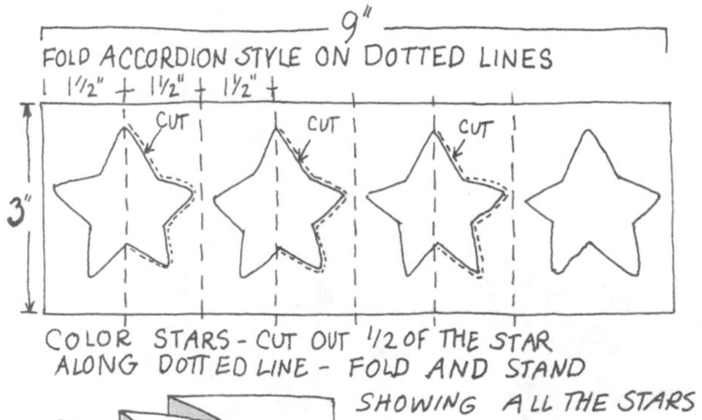

9"
FOLD ACCORDION STYLE ON DOTTED LINES
1½"   1½"   1½"
CUT   CUT   CUT
3"
COLOR STARS - CUT OUT ½ OF THE STAR
ALONG DOTTED LINE - FOLD AND STAND
SHOWING ALL THE STARS

This star card is easy to cut out yet looks very sophisticated!

HO HO HO

Make a photo collage with photographs of the children taken throughout the year. Photocopy the collage and use as holiday cards. By using colored pencils, you can achieve a tinted effect on each copy.

Buy graph paper to use as background for your card. It will provide a guide for young kids' drawings of houses and trees and aid them in forming the letters.

Use a piece of card or tagboard about 4 by 5 inches as your backing. Cut out a rectangle about 1½ by 3 inches out of wrapping paper and glue three sides down on the card (this will look like a little paper bag—you will want to leave the top open). Find a picture of a cat or puppy in a magazine and cut it out and slip the picture into the top of the bag. Write the greeting around the front of the card or include a message in the bag.

Personalize messages using rubber stamps, computers, printing kits, and stencils.

Make a tiny card and enclose it in a baby sock, which is attached to the gift.

Cut out your favorite comics and white out the words. Photocopy and then print in your own dialogue; or send the funny comic as is, with your own greeting at the end.

Decorate printed cards with your own drawings, or by adding stickers, stamps, glitter, buttons, and/or other decorative ornaments to give them your own special touch.

This dreidel turns into a three-dimensional card. Photocopy our drawing on colored paper and then fill in the Hebrew characters on each side with a colored ink (we used blue paper and gold markers). When done, fold and put together as per our instructions.

FOLD IN

T O P

PUNCH HOLE

FOLD IN

FOLD IN

FOLD IN

FOLD IN

FOLD IN

FOLD IN

TUCK

TAPE OR GLUE IN FLAP

TAPE OR GLUE

USE A PIECE OF A STRAW FOR KNOB

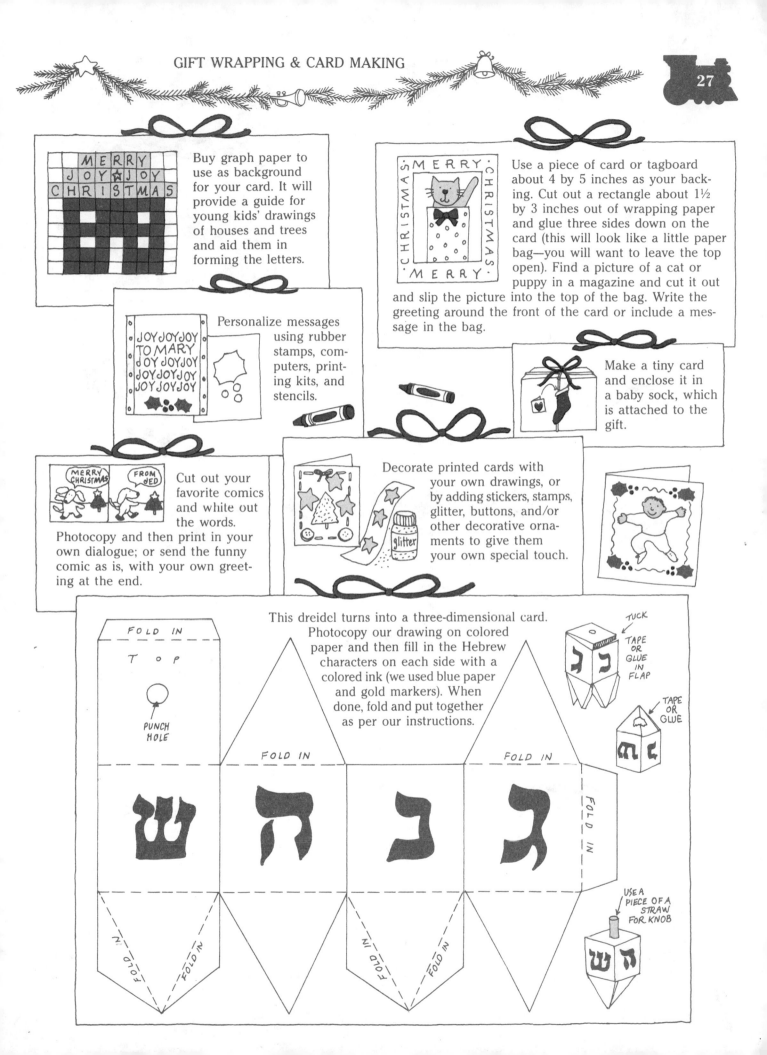

GIFT-WRAPPING

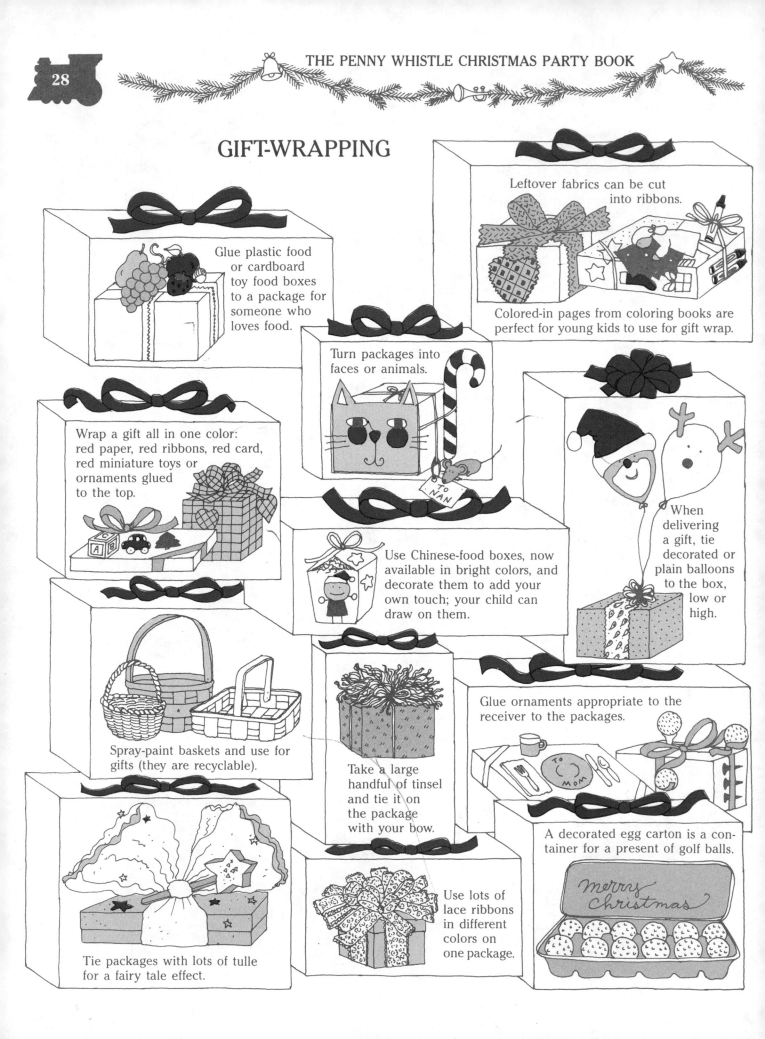

Glue plastic food or cardboard toy food boxes to a package for someone who loves food.

Leftover fabrics can be cut into ribbons.

Colored-in pages from coloring books are perfect for young kids to use for gift wrap.

Turn packages into faces or animals.

TO NAN

Wrap a gift all in one color: red paper, red ribbons, red card, red miniature toys or ornaments glued to the top.

Use Chinese-food boxes, now available in bright colors, and decorate them to add your own touch; your child can draw on them.

When delivering a gift, tie decorated or plain balloons to the box, low or high.

Spray-paint baskets and use for gifts (they are recyclable).

Take a large handful of tinsel and tie it on the package with your bow.

Glue ornaments appropriate to the receiver to the packages.

TO MOM

A decorated egg carton is a container for a present of golf balls.

Merry Christmas

Tie packages with lots of tulle for a fairy tale effect.

Use lots of lace ribbons in different colors on one package.

Instead of ribbon, use grapevines (you can get them at a farmer's market or florist); make vine wreaths and add dry flowers.

Use oversize wide ribbons and large bows on small packages.

Glue a large paper doily on one corner of the wrapped gift; glue several small doilies all over the package.

Use comics, maps, newspaper, or sheet music as wrapping paper and adorn with appropriate toys (trains, planes, musical instruments).

Gel paper in colors is great for wrapping large or unusually shaped things that don't fit into regular boxes; baskets (especially flat open ones) are also great to anchor such gifts in place (wrap gel around them).

For a fan of a particular comic strip, collect a number of strips and use them for wrapping paper.

Use a plastic waste basket covered with a Santa hat.

Turn a package into a sled, a schoolbus, a snowman, a Santa, a die.

MERRY TO

Wrap potpourri in lace and tie with ribbon.

SANTA FLIP

Tie a birthday book or holiday gift book to the gift.

Surprise wrapping: Place gifts in oddly shaped and oversized packages.

Wrap gifts in bandannas or Christmas fabric.

Use a deck of cards; glue a few on a package or cover the box.

Make awards and write "To the best . . ."; attach seals to ends of ribbons and add gold stars.

Place miniature store-bought bows in a pattern on a gift box: Make an outline of a Christmas tree, a line of bows, etc.

✳

If the gift your child wrapped is just too beautiful to ruin with the opening, cut around the bottom of the wrapping, lift off his or her special creation and save.

❄

When you are creating your own wrapping paper, make "baby" footprints by making a fist, then placing the bottom in a pan of paint, and stamping the print. Then take your thumb, dip into the paint, and place it above the fist print.

❄

Use raffia instead of ribbon to tie up a package. Then tie a Christmas ornament to finish it off.

❄

A tie-dyed paper towel idea: For each dye, place 5 drops of food coloring in ½ cup of water in a small bowl. Have your child fold an industrial-strength white paper towel to fit into his hand. Dip into a dye, refold, and place in another color. Refold again and then put into another color. When done, you have a tie-dyed piece of wrapping paper. After it dries, you can wrap a small gift in it or use it as a painting, which can be framed.

Make different papers using:

· Footprints and handprints.
· Rubber stamps.
· Gummed dots and squares on plain paper and on ribbons.
· Foil with stickers on it.
· Sponges dipped in paint on brown, recyclable, or freezer paper.
· Plain paper with stickers on it.

· Rice paper splattered with India ink and tied with grosgrain ribbons.
· Stencils are magic! Spray-paint your own designs; you can spray-paint ribbons as well (splatter the ribbons when the gift is wrapped).
· Plain wrapping paper with holes punched in it to create designs.

GROUP PRESENTS

If more than one present is going to a person, or you are giving a number of gifts to one family, try these ideas:

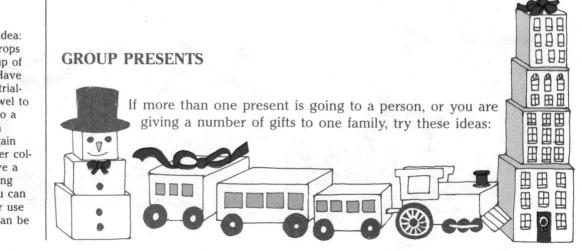

PARTIES

• When we say "you," we mean you *and* your child. Involve your child at every stage of planning. Participation and involvement in each part of the decision-making process is critical to making your child feel involved and important.

• If this is your child's first (or even second) Christmas or Hanukkah, make it a simple event rather than an elaborate celebration.

• Plan ahead! The more preparation time you can build into your schedule, the better. Finding decorations, music tapes, and items needed for games and activities all take legwork and time.

• Plan activities for every moment of the party. Think of your party as a play with a beginning, a middle, and an end. Having a complete plan will give you greater control, will minimize potential problems, and will virtually guarantee that your party will be a smash.

• Take part in the party. Don't stay in the kitchen or watch from the sidelines. Participate in the activities, in the "process" of the party, and you will be amazed at how much fun you will have and how much your children will appreciate your involvement.

• There's no doubt about it—you'll need extra hands, and your "staff" can just as easily be composed of the family's teenagers or neighbors and friends as of some hired help. Think through the jobs that will be required ahead of time. Make your assignments and notify your assistants before the party. Lists and charts are helpful here, too. Write it down, then you won't forget and your helpers have a place to look for guidance without asking you fifty times!

• Holiday festivities that include your children are the best. Whether it's organizing the beginnings of the party (including basic decision-making), designing and addressing the invitations, or deciding on the activities and menu, your children will have more of an investment in the occasion if you do it all together. Many of the activities and games included here are designed for adults and children to play together. A large number of the craft ideas can be joint projects. And even the menus include items that can be made together— some by children alone and others by everyone working together.

• All of these parties are structured so that any activity, game, decoration, or food can be easily adapted from one party to another. *Most games included in parties that have a Christmas theme can be easily adapted for a Hanukkah party.* Remember, our suggestions are just that—it is your added imagination, creativity, and requirements that will make your party uniquely yours.

SUPPLY LIST

Glue Gun
Scissors
Florist Wire
Tape
White Glue
Markers
Puff Paints
Tagboard
Glitter
Fabric
Felt
Sequins
Buttons
Lace
Cookie Cutters
Food Coloring
Tracing Paper
Beads
Tissue Paper
Ribbons

• You will find that there are probably more games suggested for a party than you will need. That's because we've discovered that being prepared is better than being caught with extra time on your hands. You probably won't have time to play every game or take part in every activity, but you will have greater peace of mind.

• Take photographs! The whole family will want to remember the party, but all too often the taking of pictures gets lost in the excitement of the event. Assign this task to one of your helpers. If you have a video camera, take movies and then play them back before the children leave. Instant snapshots are good for immediate gratification.

• Creating the appropriate atmosphere is particularly important when planning a Christmas or Hanukkah party. In the *Penny Whistle Party Planner,* we suggested that, when it comes to decorating parties, less is more—that overdecorating is unnecessary and may, in fact, overwhelm your child. But many people will disagree when it comes to Christmas and Hanukkah. Decorations seem to accumulate over the years and become traditions in themselves, particularly when children make ornaments that grow more valuable as the children grow older. There is often an air of excitement for kids in simply bringing down the box of holiday decorations from the top shelf of the closet and placing these family treasures around the house, as well as handing down decorations from generation to generation.

• Invitations set the stage and mood for the party. Make them inventive and send them three weeks ahead of time, if at all possible. Each party in this book has a suggested invitation or two. Some have drawings you can photocopy. Don't hesitate to add your own personal touch to these invitations, or to choose an invitation from one party and adapt it to another.

• At the end of each party, you will find a menu with the corresponding recipes at the end of the book. Again, these are suggestions. If you want to switch dishes from one party to another, you can do so easily. And if you are overwhelmed with plans and would rather order a pizza, do it! Keep in mind that giving a party is supposed to be easy and fun, so whenever you are faced with a decision and the easier road beckons, go ahead and take it!

Be prepared for the unexpected:
· Make additional invitations in case some don't get delivered or you need to "add on" at the last minute.
· Have a cushion of extra food, drinks, favors, props.
· Have a fire extinguisher in the house and in working order (particularly if you are using candles for decorations).

SANTA'S WORKSHOP

Here is a holiday party that emphasizes gift *giving* instead of gift *getting*. It gives the children a chance to make gifts for their parents and friends, and it offers you a chance to say "thanks" to those parents who have helped you during the year by giving them a few free hours during this busy season.

   If you schedule this party about three weeks before the holidays, the children can plan on making these gifts for their parents and friends. You also want the parents to know that they will have this free time so they can make their plans accordingly (if you plan the party on a Saturday, it will give parents a practical time to do their own holiday shopping while you supervise the kids). Three hours may be about right for this event.

INVITATION

This is a small gift-wrapped box, tied with a tiny Santa or a candy cane, with the invitation inside:

You are Invited to
SANTA'S WORKSHOP
BRING YOUR HOLIDAY GIFT LIST
and give the folks an afternoon off!
Come to the Bailey's at noon on
DEC. 8th - 234 HORN LANE
please let us know you are coming
~ CALL 555-1234 ~

When you send gifts through the mail, once-beautiful bows are often crushed, making for sad children's faces. Try omitting the bow, substituting your own designs and pictures, and gluing them flat on the packages.

ACTIVITIES

Have one card table set aside for each activity. You can also set aside one table for wrapping finished gifts with boxes of different sizes, wrapping paper, ribbons, glue and tape, scissors, as well as a variety of cards the kids can use or make. (See Gift Wrapping and Card Making, page 24.)

MERRY

GIFT CERTIFICATES

These are gift certificates for a particular service. Use 8½-by-11-inch construction paper for backing. Glue typing paper trimmed to 7 by 10 inches to the colored paper. Draw a certificate trim on it (see drawing), leaving room for a pledge written in the child's handwriting. Have the kids fill out the certificates for whatever gifts they are giving their parents. Remember, time and service are perfect gifts. Some examples:

"I will walk the dog every morning for a month."
"I will baby-sit."
"I will repair five things."
"I will give you a day."
"I will serve breakfast in bed on three Sundays."

FOR GRANDMA
I will walk your dog every morning for a month

Add a gold seal—and you're done. As a last-minute alternative, buy ready-made gift certificates at any stationery store.

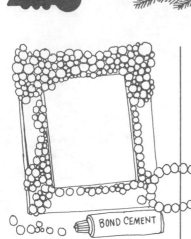

PICTURE FRAMES WITH JEWELS

Get all sizes and colors of pearls (or mix them with other beads) from a bead store, and some Bond™ 527 Multi Purpose Cement. Glue each pearl onto a Plexiglas or wood frame, piling the pearls one on the other, forming mounds of pearls at the corners. You can also buy inexpensive bead necklaces at craft and bead shops and glue these on.

❋

Rainbow stamp pads make beautiful images with any rubber stamp.

MEMO PADS

Get an assortment of rubber stamps, including a set of all the letters of the alphabet, and stamp pads in different ink colors. At the stationery store, buy inexpensive notepads in different colors. Each child can stamp a pad with a name or a message on each page of the pad for a personalized gift.

FLOWERPOTS

Buy some clay pots, potting soil, and a flat of flowering plants, at the local nursery. The children can spray-paint the pots and even stencil names on them. You may want to help them actually plant the flowers in each pot. The finished gifts can be wrapped in cellophane and tied with ribbon or raffia.

❋

Gift-wrap plants in tissue paper so they don't suffocate.

❋

Tiny wooden hearts, stars, triangles, and other shapes are available in packages at craft shops. They can be glued onto the jewelry boxes for a three-dimensional effect.

JEWELRY BOXES

Children love boxes—even if they never use them, they love to decorate them and give them as gifts. Buy wooden boxes with hinges and latches at a hobby shop (or you can use cardboard boxes of different sizes). Have acrylic paints (thin them out so they dry fast), stickers, and beads and buttons in bowls on the table. Buy small springs at the hardware store; you can glue a larger bead or jewel on top of a spring and then glue the spring to the cover of the box.

Variations: You can make a Junk Box: cover with bottle caps, newspaper comics, pieces of sponge, old keys, twigs, rubber bands, tea bags, paper clips or fasteners, any plastic objects; or choose a holiday theme and make the appropriate box.

❋

To glue a bead to your jewelry box or picture frame, insert the bead on the end of a toothpick until it fits tightly. Put the glue on your project, place the bead carefully with the toothpick, and hold the bead down with your fingertips as you remove the toothpick. You can also use eyebrow tweezers.

SNOW GLOBES

Obie Slamon makes snow globes from jam and jelly jars. Here's how: hard-boil two eggs per jar. Peel each egg and put the eggshell on a paper towel. Holding each eggshell under running water, carefully remove the inner layer of skin, leaving only the clean shell (it doesn't matter if the shell breaks—you want it in little pieces anyway). Place the shells of two eggs per jar in the food processor and process until the eggshells are tiny (you can also do this by hand with a wooden mallet).

Have mineral oil, the prepared eggshells, and miniature plastic toys ready. Have each child place his jar open side up and fill with mineral oil. Now add the crushed shells to the mineral oil in the jar.

Choose as many miniature toys as you have children (by miniature we mean really tiny—they have to fit on the lids of the jars). Each child then glues one toy with the glue gun (or with Bond™ 527 Multi Purpose Cement glue) to the inside top cover of the jar. Let dry for 15 minutes. Now you can tightly screw the lid to the jar that has been filled with the mineral oil and crushed eggshells and turn over. That's the globe!

❄ Some of the best presents don't involve money. A gift of a repair job or a maintenance offer is sometimes the most appreciated gift.

❄ Wrap presents in misleadingly shaped and sized boxes with confusing tags such as "Don't Squeeze," "Open Carefully," "Keep Level."

BAKING BEADS

These beads are baked from Sculpture Clay by Sculpey. You get ten bricks of clay in one package of ten different colors (about ten dollars). Each brick makes about eighteen to twenty beads.

First break off pieces the size of marbles and roll between your hands to form into beads. Use a toothpick to poke a hole right through each. You can leave each bead plain or paint with a tiny brush using acrylic tempera paint. You can combine two colors of clay in one bead and use permanent markers to make drawings or patterns.

Preheat your oven to 350°F. Bake bunches of beads on a cookie sheet for 20 minutes. Remove from the oven and let cool (they continue to harden as they are cooling). String the beads on heavy elastic thread. You can make necklaces, bracelets, and earrings.

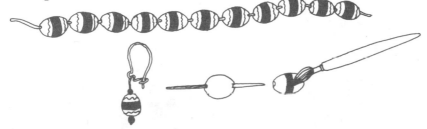

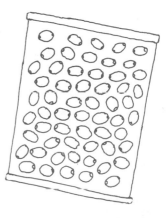

❄️
Draw a picture on paper with a marker pen, cut it out, and laminate it. Glue a pin fastener on the back for an instant pin. Poke holes and pull ear wires through for earrings.

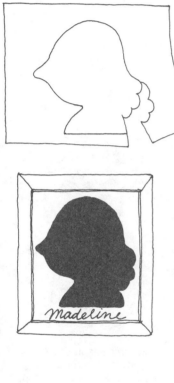

SILHOUETTE PORTRAITS

These are thoughtful gifts for family members, ones that will be saved for years to come. Follow these steps for easy results:

First have the child sit on a chair sideways against the wall. Tape white paper on the wall behind the child's face (so his face is within the outline). Have a lamp without a shade on this side of the child. When lit, it will make a shadow on the wall. Now have an adult draw the outline of the shadow face with a pencil on the paper. Have the child then cut out the outline of his face and glue it on a sheet of 8½-by-11-inch black construction paper. He then cuts it out in black and glues it on white paper.

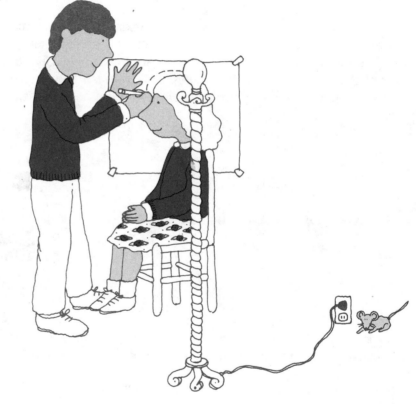

BELL NECKLACES

Place all these items on an activity table:

Packages of gold bells (found at craft and hobby shops) in various sizes; you can use several sizes or just one size.

Gold wire on a spool.

Several yards of chains made of gold plastic balls (allow one yard of chain for each necklace).

Several scissors.

Each child cuts off either 2 or 3 feet of the golden chain (the plastic is easily cut with any scissors). Take either one, two, or three bells and string them onto a piece of the gold wire about 3 inches long. The wire is then wrapped around the two ends of the gold chain, tying them together (leave about an inch of the ends hanging). The result is a gold bell necklace.

HOLIDAY BELL PLACE MATS

Children love to make place mats because they can actually be used. Bell place mats are especially popular because they are not as thematic as other Christmas place mats and can be used all year round. Bells can also be used in Hanukkah place mats (or you can use more traditional Hanukkah images).

Start by using colored construction paper (it is the right size—8½ by 11 inches or 9 by 13 inches—for a child's place mat and needs no preparation), tagboard, or larger paper, which should be cut into the appropriate size. The place mat can be this rectangular size or can be cut into a large bell.

Now collect bell stickers, bell cutouts (from holiday cards, wrapping paper, or magazines), and gold confetti (it comes in shapes of stars or circles) and glue these anywhere on the place mat. Tiny bells can be glued around the edges. Have plenty of doilies and other shiny and glossy papers in golds and silvers. You can use bell cookie cutters that can be traced and the shapes cut out. These bell cutouts are glued onto the place mat.

When done, cut out clear contact paper, with the backing still on, in the same size and shape as the place mat. Remove the backing carefully and then cover the decorated place mat. This will hold all the glued designs in place and make the place mat easy to wipe clean.

❈

Pamela Belknap recycles Christmas cards and makes collages for place mats. She divides them into different categories—religious, caricatures, Santas, angels, and so on. She pastes them on construction paper and covers the result with clear contact paper, and then binds the place mats with bias tape.

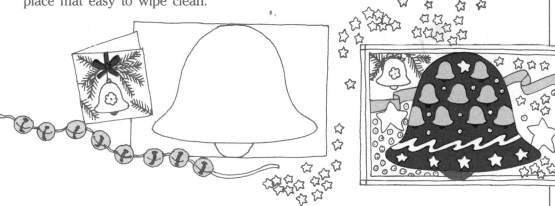

POMANDER BALLS

"What's that?" asked Annie's ten-year-old son, Marc. "It's an orange covered with cloves," she explained. "They're pretty and fill the air with the smell of cinnamon wherever you put them." "Aha!" he answered. "Can I write my name in cloves?"

And thus our individualized Pomander Ball was born. Most Pomander Balls are made when an orange or an apple are covered with cloves of cinnamon by pushing each clove right into the core until the entire fruit is completely covered. To personalize your Pomander Ball, just shape the cloves in the name you want to write. You can also make any other design on the orange (draw an outline first so it will be easier for your child to follow the design) or cover it completely with the cloves. Roll the balls in powdered orris root (available in health food stores).

❈

To make it easier to place the cloves in the orange, first poke holes with a knitting needle.

❈

A great mix to roll eight balls in is 4 tablespoons each ground cinnamon and ground cloves, 2 tablespoons each nutmeg and allspice, ¼ teaspoon ground ginger, and orris root. Leave this mixture on the balls for a week, turning them every day.

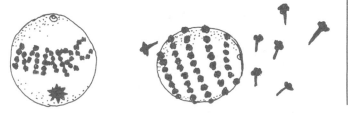

POTPOURRI

These gifts are easy to make and lovely to receive, and children feel so important when they have created a gift that they have seen selling for lots of money at the store!

Buy different varieties of potpourri. Have each child put ¼ cup of the potpourri into a 6-inch-square piece of lace. Fold it up and tie with a ribbon. These can be gifts for Mom to place in a drawer or they can be given as ornaments.

Make "faux" potpourri by filling a square of lace with straw packing material and adding a few drops of cinnamon or pine scent. Tie with a ribbon and a twig of evergreen. It smells absolutely heavenly!

SOCKS OR PAINTERS' HATS

Buy some inexpensive socks in different sizes. Have the children sew and/or glue lace, buttons, or rhinestones on them, or paint them with fabric paint. Do the same thing to painters' hats, available in paint stores (they cost about $1.50 each).

MENU

This menu is simple, because after preparing all these gift-making activities, the last thing you want to do is cook! Have the pizza delivered and make the cookies ahead of time.

Pizza (you can decorate it with green and red peppers, forming the shape of a tree)

*Perfect Holiday Cookies

*Cranapple Punch

*See recipes on page 112.

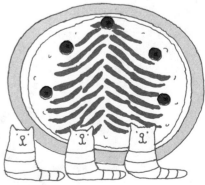

TREE-TRIMMING PARTY

Legend tells us that it was Martin Luther who, after walking in the snow and seeing a snow-covered tree reflecting the light of the stars above, first decorated a tree in his home at Christmas by placing candles on the branches. Queen Victoria of England took decorating the tree a step further by adding baubles to hers. Many Christmases later, the candles have been replaced by strings of light, strings of fruit have been replaced by garlands of popcorn and cranberries, and hanging apples have been replaced by glass balls. Angels on the tree remind us of the angels who witnessed Christ's birth, and the star at the top of the tree represents the star that guided the shepherds to Bethlehem.

❄️
The perfect ornament for young kids to make: Crumble aluminum foil into a ball. Stick fingers in spots to give it shape and it will reflect light.

Today's trees are decorated with hundreds of different ornaments, and trimming the Christmas tree together with family and friends has become a memory to treasure. For children, making ornaments and hanging them on a tree with their friends is an extra-special treat, an evening they'll always remember. Our Tree-Trimming Party is actually two parties, allowing both the adults and the children to make their own ornaments and decorate their own trees. If you can, set aside a smaller tree just for the children, as well as tables full of craft and art supplies that they can make into ornaments. It makes them feel very special to decorate their own tree any way they like, with ornaments they themselves have made. Having a couple of teenagers available to supervise can make the event progress more smoothly.

INVITATION

This three-layered card has see-through cutouts on the first two pieces.

❄️
Children love to see multiples of things. If you are planning to have an extra tree, especially a small one, you can make a "one-ornament" tree. Try a patriotic tree all in red, white, and blue with flags, or one with gingerbread hands, or one with all angels or bells or stars.

INVITATION INSTRUCTIONS

1. Photocopy our drawings on two pieces of paper: The first page should be on red paper, the second on green. Then write your own information (with your name and address) on a third piece of paper and photocopy it on white or yellow paper.

2. Cut out the outlined parts with an X-acto knife™. Use a hole puncher for the circles (you could also use a star puncher).

3. Use a gold fastener to hold the card together. You could also close it with a gold pipe cleaner or a matching ribbon.

DECORATIONS

At this party, the "decorations" are the two trees—one for the adults and the other for the children. Dinner is buffet style, so decorate the table as you would for any Christmas party. For a centerpiece that the children can help make, core twelve apples and stick 1-inch-thick, 12-inch-high candles in each center. It's a novel centerpiece that can be embellished with greens, bows, glass balls, holly, or flowers.

ACTIVITIES

Making ornaments and decorating the trees is the center of this party. After everyone is finished, or even while the decorating is going on, some children may feel restless and want to play some games. At the end of the ornament-making section, you will find some diversions that are fun either when the ornament making is completed or as others are still making ornaments and decorating the trees.

CHILDREN'S TREE

Family parties always need to include children's activities, and having a separate tree for the children to decorate by themselves is an important part of this evening. The children's tree can be smaller than the adult tree, with its own supply of ornaments that the children can hang and/or make. Have the lights already strung since this is usually not the "fun" part for little kids and requires supervision. Plan some "decorating" games, such as *stringing popcorn*. (Stringing popcorn can be quite frustrating, especially for a small child, but it is such a popular holiday activity that we always feel compelled to include at least one short string on our tree.) Sometimes, making a game out of the task takes a bit of the frustration out, so give each child a 3-foot-long double thread with a needle at one end and a knot at the other. Award a prize for the child who finishes first (one appropriate gift is an extra ornament the child can take home to put on his tree).

❋ Use green florist wire to hang ornaments. It is very pliable and easy to work with and the green color disappears among the tree branches.

❋ If your child has made several Christmas decorations at school or at home, hang one on each door in the house, not just on the front door. He will appreciate this extra touch.

❋ To estimate how many lights you need on your Christmas tree, multiply the height of the tree times the width of the tree at its widest part times 3. For example, an 8-foot tree that is 5 feet wide, times 3, would hold approximately 120 lights.

❅
Put dates on the ornaments that you make so you will remember when they were made.

❅
Storing bread dough ornaments: Be careful to store these in a tin container because any moisture will turn them to mush!

❅
You'd be surprised at what craft stores carry on their shelves. There are all sorts of items you can paint and decorate—even small wooden cutouts with moving parts that can be painted and hung as decorations on your tree or from your mantel.

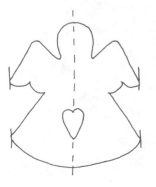

ORNAMENTS

We have come a long way from the days in Germany, over 300 years ago, when people decorated their trees by hanging apples and cookies from the branches. Well, maybe not such a long way, because today, all those years later, cookies are still a popular tree ornament, especially among children. But there are many more.

Families pass on ornaments from generation to generation, often amassing priceless collections that delight celebrants every year. Children, in particular, adore making and hanging ornaments, and take special delight in hanging ornaments they made last year while creating new ones.

For all these children, both young and old, we have assembled an assortment of ornaments from our own homes, from our family traditions, from the collections of our friends and neighbors, and from our own inspirations. And what they all have in common is that they can be made by children and adults, alone or together, both before Christmas and during the Tree-Trimming Party. To hang ornaments with friends is a real treat for children; to be able to hang ornaments they actually made with their own hands, together with their friends, is even more memorable.

The ornaments below are listed and explained simply. Most often it is obvious what supplies you and your child will need; when not, we list them. Remember, when we say "decorate," we mean with glitter, sequins, beads, paints, buttons, feathers, or anything else that appeals to you.

There are several ways to organize this ornament-making activity. You and your child can choose one ornament and make many of that one—that can result in a tree full of Gingerbread Men, each one decorated a little differently or perhaps personalized with each guest's name. Should you choose this route, we suggest making the Gingerbread Men with your child *the day before* the party. Then, at the party, you and your guests can decorate the cookies and hang them together.

Or you can choose several ornaments and plan to make one of each at the party. Look over the list you have put together and see which ornaments require some preparation, so that things that need to be baked or dried overnight will not surprise you that day. By reading through the entire list with your child and choosing which ornaments he would love to make, you can then compile one supply list and place the items on one "supply table" so the children can have the items they need within easy reach when making the ornaments.

Whichever you choose to do, work *with* your child—not only because it is fun, but also because it is safer.

Gingerbread Men or Hands—

Whether you choose to make a tree full of only Gingerbread Men or Gingerbread Hands, or choose to scatter these ornaments among others you make, you will have to make these ahead of time. Just follow the directions on page 19 and decorate with icing designs or names.

Balls and Variations—

Use commercial ornament balls—colored, clear plastic, or glass—and have your child create his own variations. Try:

- Wrapping a ball in fabric or lace and tying at the top with a ribbon;
- Pulling off the top and inserting a mini flag or a message (wrap with the words on the outside so it is readable) or sequins;
- Pouring 1 teaspoon of acrylic paint into the ball and swirling it around;
- Personalizing each ball by writing a name or making a design with glitter pens;
- Sticking tiny stars or circle stickers all over the ornament.

Items to Decorate—

Dip in paint and glitter, spray-paint and/or decorate pinecones, clothespins, wooden eggs, wood spools, wooden cutouts (found at hobby shops), wood letters.

Garlands—

Kids find chains easy to make because they just have to repeatedly string an item together. Other than popcorn, try stringing decorative buttons, pretzels, or cranberries. You can also cut out people, angels, or snowflake chains.

Cornucopias—

Make a cone from a square piece of paper (plain or wrapping) and glue to close. Line the outside top rim with ribbon and make a loop for hanging. Decorate and fill with *tiny* candies (large pieces will be too heavy and it will break).

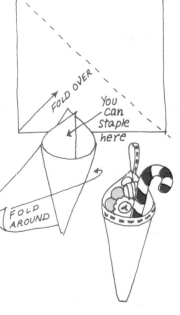

Potpourri—

Fill lace doilies or lace and netting with a tablespoon of potpourri and tie with ribbons or different color lace.

Gifts—

Empty matchboxes and wrap with wrapping paper and tie with ribbon.

Miniature Baskets—Spray-paint them and fill with straw flowers or candy.

Masks—You can decorate plain half masks: Make a Santa mask (a red mask with a white beard and moustache from cotton) or a glamorous mask with red and green feathers and sequins.

Bows—Collect all sizes and colors of ribbons and tie in bows. These are particularly great for young kids because they make simple ornaments. Very large bows tied all over the tree also look great!

Copper Animals—Place an animal cookie cutter on a copper sheet, trace, and cut with a scissor. Punch a hole, tie a ribbon, and hang. These ornaments should be made with adult supervision.

Porcelain Faces—Porcelain angels, Santas, and masks are available in hobby stores. Just paint with acrylic paints.

Felt—Trace shapes from cookie cutters on felt and cut out two of each shape. Glue together leaving a 1-inch opening; decorate with beads or sequins or other fabric decorations (you can use a glue gun); stuff with polyfill and glue the opening shut. Attach a hanging cord or ribbon with a needle and heavy thread.

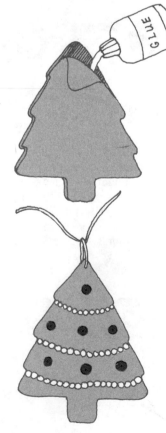

Wire Fantasies—Take a piece of fishing wire and shape around various cookie cutters. Carefully remove the wire, dip in white glue and then glitter. Let dry and hang.

Doilies—Just plain doilies are perfect for tiny tots to hang right on the tree. Since they are usually white, they look just like snowflakes. In gold and silver, they look like fancy ornaments.

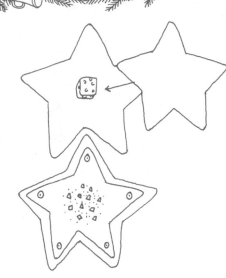

Stars—For each star, trace a star-shaped cookie cutter on two pieces of hard shiny cardboard (gold or silver) or plain cardboard covered with mylar or other shiny wrapping paper, and cut out. Glue a 1-inch-square piece of sponge in the middle of one star and glue the other onto that one, creating stars that are three-dimensional. You can also make one star slightly smaller than the other for a "shadow" effect.

Mirrors—Buy a variety of flat mirror ornaments and have your child paint and decorate them. He can write his name on them using tube paints or paint his own design on them.

Clothespins—There are miniature clothespins called Dollipins (Penley Corp., W. Paris, Maine 04289—you get fifty for $2.75). Dip first into paint, and then glitter, and, when dry, fasten onto the tree.

Pasta Chains—Collect various sizes of tube macaroni, heavy string, and big-eyed needles (those used for carpet weaving are best for kids to use because they are blunt). Spray-paint the macaroni, and string into a colorful chain. This is great for younger kids who find stringing popcorn or cranberries too difficult.

Twig stars—Make a star out of twigs and tie together with raffia.

Mini Houses—Photocopy our house below on colored paper, color in, fold as illustrated, glue, decorate to your taste, and hang.

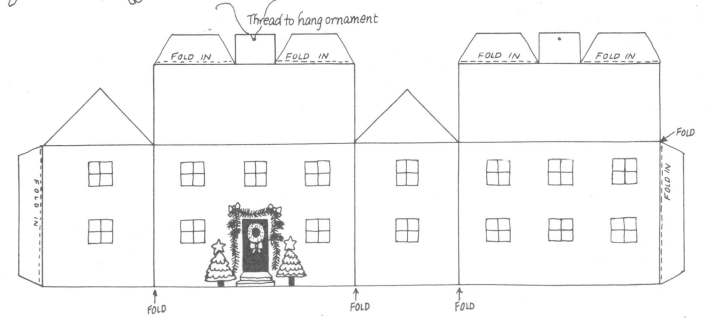

Thread to hang ornament

FOLD IN   FOLD IN   FOLD IN   FOLD IN

FOLD

FOLD IN   FOLD IN

FOLD   FOLD   FOLD

Stained Glass Windows—For the easiest stained glass windows, try to buy cookie cutters in the same shapes but in different sizes. For example, if you want stained glass windows with hearts, buy a 4-inch heart-shaped cookie cutter and another that is 2 inches. You can use hearts, stars, Santas, trees, bells, among others. Use either the Perfect Holiday Cookies recipe (page 112) or the Gingerbread Dough (page 19) for these. Cut out the larger shape, then use the smaller cutter to cut out a "hole" in the center. Use a chopstick, pencil tip, or straw to make a hole for hanging.

To make the stained glass, crush hard candies in different colors. Place the window shape on a greased cookie sheet and fill the "hole" with crushed candy. Bake for about 8 minutes. Remove and let cool. When cool, remove from the cookie sheet and thread with ribbon through the hole. The stained glass ornament is ready to hang.

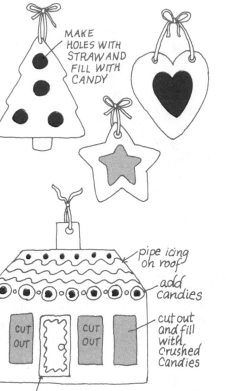

MAKE HOLES WITH STRAW AND FILL WITH CANDY

pipe icing on roof

add candies

cut out and fill with crushed candies

CUT OUT   CUT OUT

pipe on a door with icing

Flag ornaments—For your patriotic child, use red, white, and blue ribbons to make bows, and place around the tree. To carry out the theme, glue miniature flags to paper cutouts and hang; make a chain out of red, white, and blue beads (there are even star beads that you can add). Look for ribbons and wrapping paper that have flag motifs on them.

Gourds—Miniature gourds are easy to paint. When dry (they dry very fast) make a hole through the top and hang with a ribbon.

Wood Shavings—These come in bags at hobby shops in natural or stained colors. You can make them into chains (just glue or staple into each other) or hang separately on the tree.

WHITE BEAD

Ping-Pong Ball Santa—Use a Ping-Pong ball and paint the top half red for hat; paint eyes (or stick eye stickers on); glue a cotton ball on the bottom for the beard. Make a hole through the ball with a long sewing needle and hang with an ornament hanger.

Mini Trees—Cut little trees out of green construction paper or felt and decorate (here little beads, jewels, and stickers work beautifully). You can also buy bags of miniature brush trees and wreaths (green or white), and spray with gold paint or glue and then dip into a cup full of glitter or sequins. Stick the tree into a cork, tie a ribbon to the top, and hang.

Mini Christmas Stockings—Decorate baby socks and fill with lightweight candies.

Bread Dough—Remember, this dough is *not* for eating.

Baker's Clay
4 cups unsifted all-purpose flour
1 cup salt
1½ cups cold water

Preheat the oven to 350°F.

Stir together the flour, salt, and water until everything is well blended. Turn the dough out onto a lightly floured board and knead vigorously for about 5 minutes until a smooth, pliable, nonsticky dough is formed. Add some more flour to the board if necessary to prevent sticking in the early stages of kneading. The finished dough should not be sticky.

Break off the dough in small portions as you use it, keeping the rest in a plastic bag to prevent it from drying out. Roll out the dough and transfer to a cookie sheet. Cut into shapes with cookie cutters. Be sure to create a hole for the string that will support the ornament by piercing the dough on top with a chopstick, pencil tip, or straw.

Bake the shapes for 50 to 60 minutes or until they feel solid and are ivory to light brown in color. Cool. Decorate or paint with acrylic paints and spray with shellac.

Note: The dough should be baked within 4 to 5 hours of making it. The yield depends on the sizes of your figures.

Walnut Strawberries—Paint walnuts red and glue green felt leaves on top. You can paint white dots on them for an extra-realistic touch.

Balsa Wood—Trace shapes from cookie cutters on pieces of balsa wood ¹⁄₁₆ inch thick (candy canes, letters, houses, snowflakes, animals, and the like work great). Cut out with large scissors and paint. Punch a hole and hang with raffia.

Cranberry Hearts (or any shape)—Mold florist wire around a cookie cutter to get the shape you want; remove, and string the cranberries on the wire.

Airplane—Take a wooden clothespin, place two toothpicks across the top for the propellers, a wooden ice-cream stick through the clothespin for the wings, and you have an airplane. Spray with spray paint.

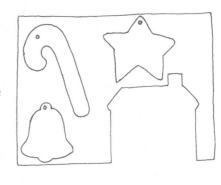

❄

When you make your Gingerbread Hands, add rings on the fingers with frosting and small candies.

❄

Collect or buy samples of wood moldings (they are inexpensive and easily available in lumberyards or hardware stores)—the more ornate, the better—and other leftover finished pieces of wood. By gluing the pieces together, you will create one-of-a-kind wooden ornaments. You can leave them plain or paint them.

❄

Use the backs of plastic spoons for faces of dolls or angels. Attach pipe cleaners for arms; paper, cloth, or lace for a simple dress. Draw a face on the plastic spoon.

GAMES FOR ADULTS AND CHILDREN

Hidden Christmas Treasures

This magical mystery tree is full of hidden treasures. Distribute a copy of this picture to each child. The kids can play several games with this one drawing. Have everyone look for things that begin with the letter *s* and then the letter *c* (see the lists below). Next have them find objects that have something to do with Christmas, or list the "toys" hidden in the tree.

Items that begin with *s*:		Items that begin with *c*:	
Santa	snowman	car	crown
snowflake	sweater	cap	comb
sock	skis	calendar	candy
stocking	sailboat	cage	cookies
scarf	snake	cake	cat
star	skate	carrot	cup
sled	scissors	coin	crocodile

Lights Out

This game is fun to play, but it does need supervision.

On an empty table covered with a plastic cloth (to protect the table from dripping wax), arrange five to seven tall candles, well fastened into short candle holders. Arrange the candles at different distances from one end of the table. The blowing line is at one end—for example, one candle would be 1½ feet away from the blowing line, another at 2 feet, a third at 2½ feet, the fourth at 3 feet, and so on. Assign a different point value to each candle—the closest one to the blowing line would be worth the lowest number of points.

Allow each player 15 seconds to blow out the candles (be sure an adult relights the candles after each turn). Award a prize to the child who gets the most points.

Take a toy ladder and lean it against your Christmas tree. Place a stuffed elf or Santa Claus walking up the ladder.

❄

Herb Long of West Dover, Vermont, believes in cutting down an ugly tree for his family's Christmas tree. He then cuts off the branches and glues them to a dowel to make a perfectly symmetrical tree. His philosophy: Why cut down a perfect tree, which should be left to thrive in nature?

BEGIN FLIPBOOK HERE!

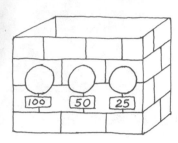

Down the Chimney

Draw bricks with a wide black marker on an approximately 4-by-3-foot piece of cardboard so it will look like a chimney. Cut out three holes about 5 inches round. Place a number under each for points—try 25 for one, 50 for another, and 100 for the last. Hand out small beanbags or Ping-Pong balls, three to a child. The object is for the child to get as many points as he can. You can have each child try his hand at this game or separate the kids into teams.

Skating Race

Place three bowls of ice cubes on separate chairs at one end of the room and three empty bowls on three chairs at the other end of the room. Each player takes off his shoes and gets a tablespoon. Each player "skates" (slides) back and forth, carrying the ice cubes one at a time to the empty bowl; the object of the game is to empty one bowl and fill the other. If a cube is dropped, it's out of the game. When everyone is finished, the ice cubes in the bowls are counted; the player who gets the most in the bowl wins.

Presents, Presents, Everywhere

A great part of this party is making and hanging the ornaments. An added treat is to have your guests find their own gifts already hanging on the tree. Take some inexpensive and funny items, personalize them (write a name on each, making sure each guest has an ornament), and hang them on the tree—the adult's surprises on their tree and the children's surprises on their tree. Suggested gifts: combs, personalized notepads, soaps, miniature toys, cosmetic accessories, and flip books.

❄ You can color some of the popcorn with food dye the day before you string it.

❄ Our friend Mark Friedland, of Artafax in Los Angeles, mixes glitter into acrylic paints. He then takes a glass ball ornament, lifts off the top, and pours a little of this glitter paint into the ball. When the top is replaced, you can swirl the paint inside the ball to create a magical design!

MENU

*Oyster Stew
*Wassail
*Christmas Crudités
*Yule Log
*Smoked Turkey on a Stick
*Perfect Holiday Cookies

*See recipes on pages 112–113.

I'M DREAMING OF A WHITE CHRISTMAS

T he idea for this party came out of Annie's daughter Lisa's annual California-like lament that the holidays just didn't seem the same as those celebrated in other parts of the country, where snow covered the trees and the ground, and icicles hung down from rooftops. We realized that you don't have to live in California to appreciate a "winter wonderland," all-white holiday party. Even if your lawn is already covered with two feet of snow, celebrating a white Christmas is very special indeed.

And what's Christmas without caroling! Caroling fits so perfectly into the spirit of the holidays, as families sing those favorite songs to others in the neighborhood. It is especially fitting to include the children in this very "grown-up" activity, rather than leaving them at home while the adults sing.

INVITATION

This Christmas card is a white cutout of a Christmas tree. Just follow the diagram and write the copy on the succeeding pages.

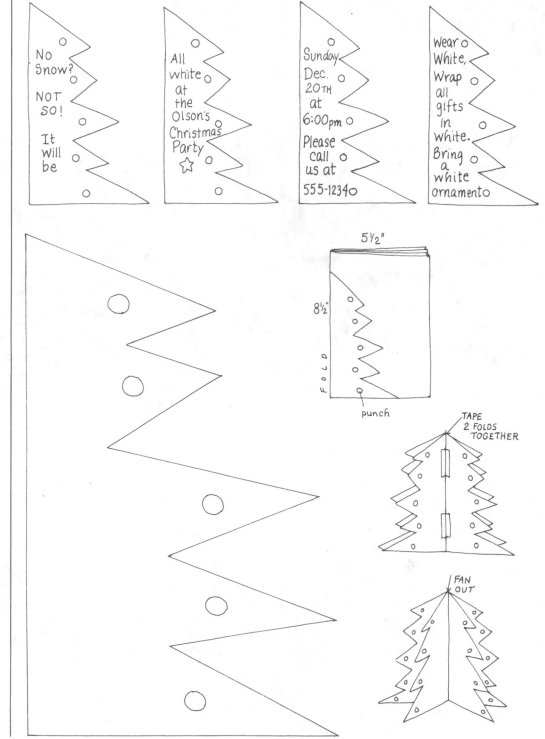

❄ You can hang stars in clusters from the ceiling the same way we hang angels.

❄ For frosted holly on her holiday table, Angela Rich freezes sprigs of holly and takes them out on Christmas Eve.

❄
Janet Surmi gives each guest a decorated, individualized grocery bag to carry the Christmas party favors home.

❄
Fluffy popcorn is ideal to use as snow cover for a table centerpiece.

DECORATIONS

An all-white decor immediately creates a winter atmosphere. It is especially appropriate for warm climates, where you can't be dependent on nature to create your winter atmosphere. This is the time to collect, design, and create everything in white. And we mean everything! Wrap the gifts that go under the tree in white paper with white ribbons. Paint your mistletoe white. Make a paper snowman with your children using white and translucent paper and hang him on the front door. Hang silver or white stars and angels from white streamers all around the house—from corners of doors, from the ceiling, from chandeliers—the works! (See page 18.) Doilies are the perfect snowflakes— already made. Have the kids collect them in all sizes and hang them from plastic thread everywhere. You can even ask your guests to dress in white.

Our canopy will be the unforgettable centerpiece of the party, where everyone gathers before caroling and later for dinner and games. Children, who love canopies and "tents" of all kinds, will find this one remaining in their memories, especially if they help to construct it. Here's how you make it:

Fasten a dowel (available at a hardware store) to each corner of the dining room table with masking, duct, or packing tape. Usually a 3-foot-long dowel is sufficient. Gather together balls of streamers or ribbons in silver or white or

the reds and greens of Christmas. (If you want to adapt this canopy for your Hanukkah table, just choose blue as your color theme and use blue ribbons or streamers). Cover each dowel with the ribbons or streamers by winding them around the stick, as you would in making a maypole. Using strong mailing tape, tape lots of ribbons or streamers (at least six per dowel) from the ceiling over the center of the table to the top of each dowel, to create a maypole effect and an instant canopy. Tape the ends of the ribbons to the top of each dowel. Now decorate the center of the canopy and the top of each corner by hanging bells, real or made from paper. If your child loves lights, string white Christmas lights from the center of the canopy or around the room. Add twigs around the cornices of the room, and string the lights and bells from the twigs.

Under the canopy, complete the scene with a "winter wonderland" table setting. Think of the centerpiece as a little diorama of a winter scene: Cover the table with a white paper tablecloth. Have the children tear the ends all around the border so it looks like icicles are hanging from the table. Get a round mirror (approximately 2 feet across) and place it at the center. Spray shaving cream around the edges or glue cotton balls all around (there is also "spray snow" available this time of the year)—and you've got an instant lake with snow on the banks. Make a Gingerbread House (page 67) and decorate with marshmallows, whipped cream, white mints, etc. Place it next to the lake. Make a path with white marshmallows. Have the children make snowmen cut out of white paper or with Ping-Pong or tennis balls.

Encourage the children to look around the house and use their imagination to add to this white wonderland. For example, white stuffed polar bears would look great around the room or on the table. White batting (cotton or polyester) can cover surfaces. The children can cover chairs and upholstered furniture with white sheets and tie with white bows. White cloth diapers can be tied in large ribbons. Remember—anything white will work!

Another option is to rent a white tent or a regular round tent and cover it with white sheets to create an instant igloo. We all know how much kids love to crawl into little houses! This "igloo" is the perfect hideaway in which the children can play games or even have a little picnic.

TAPE TO TABLE

WRAP DOWEL

Cut out silver or gold spirals from mylar and hang from the ceilings. Make them of different lengths for an effective decoration.

Di Anderson, of Piedmont, California, decorates bushy silvertip fir trees. She and her kids pop large-kernel popcorn and then throw about three garbage bags full on the trees. It stays wherever it lands and looks like snow.

ACTIVITIES

CAROLING

Place a holiday basket, all decorated with ribbons and bells, near the front door. Fill it with instruments, especially bells of different sizes in various tones, kazoos, recorders, cymbals, wood clackers, and more. As the guests come through the front door, ask them to select an instrument, which they will play when everyone goes caroling. Practicing is fun to do around your Christmas tree to get everyone in the caroling mood. (If the weather is bad, singing around the tree at home becomes the central activity.) When everyone is ready, go caroling! (For the words to some favorite carols, see page 61.) You can also play the instruments after dinner in a Christmas musicale.

When everyone returns, expect appetites to be hearty. Serving buffet style will facilitate a crowd and make it easier for you to be one of the carolers. After dinner, it's time for family games.

TIE A "WHITE, WHITE RIBBON"

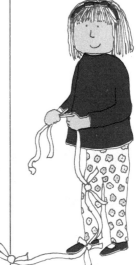

Collect half a dozen spools of white, silver, or opalescent Christmas-wrapping ribbon. Cut at least 3 dozen pieces into 12-inch lengths. Hide the pieces of ribbon all over the party room or the house. Ask the children to find as many "White, White Ribbons" as they can. As each child finds the ribbons, he has to tie them together to form a longer piece. The child with the longest ribbon at the end of the game wins. You can also hide one gold cord among the rest and give an additional prize to the child who finds that one.

PEPPERMINT PICKUPS

This is our Christmas version of pickup sticks. In the center of a table, place about a pound of hard candies. Give each child two peppermint sticks. When it is his turn, each child picks up a candy from the center pile with a peppermint stick in each hand and places it in front of him. The trick is to pick up the candy, one at a time, without moving any other candy in the pile. Not as easy as it sounds! If the candy in the pile is moved, the child loses his turn. The child with the most candy wins.

PAPER BAG PLAYERS

Each child gets a white paper bag and a felt-tip marker. He must then put the bag over his head and draw a face on the bag (obviously without looking). You give a prize to the child whose face is the clearest, then the funniest, the longest, the most unrecognizable, and so on.

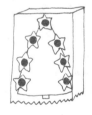

Take a paper lunch bag and lay it flat on the table. Draw the outline of a Christmas tree covering most of the bag. Draw the outline of stars around the tree. Using a hole puncher, punch holes along the outlines. When done, you have created a "luminaria," which can cover any outside lamp or light.

CHRISTMAS PENNY CAT HUNT

The object of this game is to find the right Christmas Penny Cat by reading the clues, answering the questions in the clues, and collecting all the information to come up with the right answer. Then, by the process of elimination, each child (or a group of children) finds the Christmas Penny Cat.

There are ten characteristics to notice about Penny Cat. No one Penny Cat has all of these features. Some Penny Cats have some of these characteristics, and some have others. The characteristics are:

1. He is wearing Santa's hat.
2. He has a beard.
3. He is holding a Christmas ornament.
4. He has one eye closed.
5. He is wearing snow boots.
6. He is wearing slippers.
7. He is wearing a Christmas-bell necklace.
8. He is striped.
9. He is holding a gift.
10. There is a dove on top of his hat.

Our "authentic" Christmas Penny Cat has only the following characteristics (which you keep secret from the children): He is wearing *Santa's hat*, he has a *Christmas-bell necklace* around his neck, he is wearing *slippers*, he has *both eyes open*, he is *striped*, and he is holding a *Christmas ornament*.

How do the children find the real Christmas Penny Cat? Remember, only *one* Penny Cat has the exact combination of characteristics listed above. By answering questions about Christmas and using the process of elimination, the players can come up with the right Christmas Penny Cat.

The first step is to make copies of the drawings of the ten cats above, enough to give one drawing to each guest.

The second step is to cut up clues on separate pieces of paper about 2 by 4 inches. On each slip of paper, write one question about Christmas Penny Cat

and one about Christmas to which the answers are either yes or no. If the answer to the Christmas question is yes, then the answer to the Penny Cat question is also yes; if the answer to the Christmas question is no, the answer to the Penny Cat is also no. Place all the clues in a paper bag and let the contestant take turns drawing one slip at a time. The parents read the questions.

It's easy—just see below.

Questions and Answers

1. *Is Christmas Penny Cat wearing a Santa's hat?*
   Is Christmas always on December 25? (The kids say, "Yes!")

So the answer to the top question is also yes, and the adult in charge writes that down. (Christmas Penny Cat is wearing a *Santa's hat.*) Now everyone looks at all the drawings and notes which Penny Cat is wearing a Santa's hat and eliminates the Penny Cats that aren't.

2. *Does Christmas Penny Cat have a beard?*
   Does Santa Claus live in Connecticut? (The kids say, "No.")

So the answer to the Penny Cat question is no. Christmas Penny Cat does not have a beard. The children cross out the Penny Cats that have beards.

3. *Is Christmas Penny Cat holding a Christmas ornament?*
   Did Santa check his list twice before coming to town?

The answer is yes, so we know that Christmas Penny Cat is holding an *ornament.*

4. *Does Christmas Penny Cat have one eye closed?*
   Does Santa deliver presents in a 747?

The "No" chorus will be heard all around the house. It also tells us that Christmas Penny Cat has *both eyes open.*

5. *Is Christmas Penny Cat wearing snow boots?*
   Is Scrooge excited about Christmas?

You'll get a "No" on that one, too, so we know that Christmas Penny Cat is not wearing snow boots.

If you want to play the game over and over again, just choose another one of the Penny Cats to be your Christmas Penny Cat and make up clues for that one.

6. *Is Christmas Penny Cat wearing slippers?*
Is it fun to ride in a "one horse open sleigh"?

After singing a couple of choruses of "Jingle Bells," the kids will answer, "Yes!"—so we know that Christmas Penny Cat is wearing *slippers*.

7. *Is Christmas Penny Cat wearing a Christmas-bell necklace around his neck?*
Can you put pennies inside a Christmas Stocking?

Another "Yes," so now we know that Christmas Penny Cat is wearing a *Christmas-bell necklace* around his neck.

8. *Is Christmas Penny Cat holding a gift?*
Do you "deck the halls" with poison ivy?

That "No" will be quick in coming. Now we know that Christmas Penny Cat is not holding a gift.

9. *Is there a dove on top of Christmas Penny Cat's head?*
Is it safe to light candles and hang them on the tree?

"No" to that one, so we know that there is no dove on top of Christmas Penny Cat's head.

10. *Does our Christmas Penny Cat have stripes?*
Was Blitzen a reindeer?

"Yes" to that one, so we know Christmas Penny Cat has *stripes*.

Now we know everything about Christmas Penny Cat, and the children can pick out which is the real Christmas Penny Cat.

Ann Connell Bergin turns her home into a Christmas Wonderland of dolls. She decorates a magnificent doll house with wreaths, garlands, a tiny tree and mini candy canes. There are dolls parading through her home in appropriate costumes, and antique Santa dolls that Ann has collected over the years displayed throughout.

MENU

Try to have as many white foods as you can in this white dessert buffet!

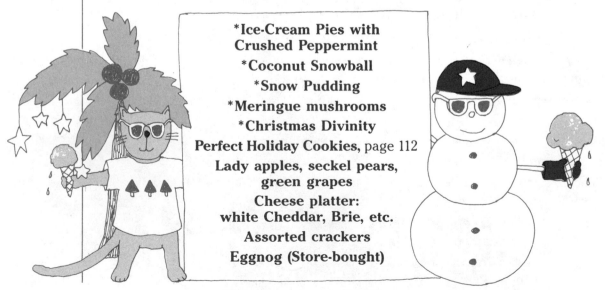

*Ice-Cream Pies with Crushed Peppermint
*Coconut Snowball
*Snow Pudding
*Meringue mushrooms
*Christmas Divinity
Perfect Holiday Cookies, page 112
Lady apples, seckel pears, green grapes
Cheese platter: white Cheddar, Brie, etc.
Assorted crackers
Eggnog (Store-bought)

*See recipes on pages 114–116.

CHRISTMAS CAROLS KIDS LOVE TO SING

WE WISH YOU A MERRY CHRISTMAS

We wish you a Merry Christmas,
We wish you a Merry Christmas,
We wish you a Merry Christmas
And a Happy New Year!

Good tidings we bring
For you and your kin.
We wish you a Merry Christmas
And a Happy New Year!

SILENT NIGHT

Silent Night! Holy Night!
All is calm, all is bright.
Round yon Virgin Mother and Child,
Holy Infant, so tender and mild,
Sleep in heavenly peace,
Sleep in heavenly peace!

Silent Night! Holy Night!
Shepherds quake at the sight!
Glories stream from heaven afar,
Heavenly hosts sing, "Alleluia!"
Christ, the Savior, is born!
Christ, the Savior, is born!

HARK! THE HERALD ANGELS SING

Hark! the herald angels sing,
"Glory to the newborn King.
Peace on earth, and mercy mild,
God and sinners reconciled."
Joyful, all ye nations rise,
Join the triumph of the skies;
With th'angelic host proclaim,
"Christ is born in Bethlehem."
Hark! the herald angels sing.
"Glory to the newborn King!"

DECK THE HALL

Deck the hall with boughs of holly,
Fa la la la la, la la la la.
'Tis the season to be jolly,
Fa la la la la, la la la la.
Don we now our gay apparel,
Fa la la, la la la, la la la.
Troll the ancient Yule-tide carol,
Fa la la la la, la la la la.

See the blazing Yule before us,
Fa la la la la, la la la la.
Strike the harp and join the chorus,
Fa la la la la, la la la la.
Follow me in merry measure,
Fa la la, la la la, la la la.
While I tell of Yule-tide treasure,
Fa la la la la, la la la la.

JINGLE BELLS

Dashing through the snow,
In a one horse open sleigh,
O'er the fields we go,
Laughing all the way!
Bells on bobtail ring,
Making spirits bright,
What fun it is to ride and sing
A sleighing song tonight!

Chorus: Jingle bells! Jingle bells!
* Jingle all the way!*
Oh, what fun it is to ride in a
* one-horse open sleigh!*
(Repeat)

❄ Christmas is a great time to play games with all members of the family. Get Parcheesi, Checkers, Dominoes, Monopoly, Lotto, and Scrabble down from the shelves.

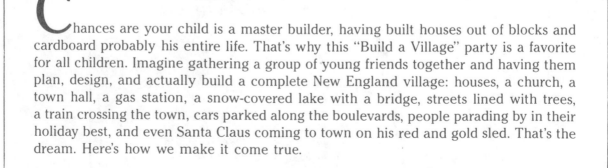

BUILD A VILLAGE PARTY

Chances are your child is a master builder, having built houses out of blocks and cardboard probably his entire life. That's why this "Build a Village" party is a favorite for all children. Imagine gathering a group of young friends together and having them plan, design, and actually build a complete New England village: houses, a church, a town hall, a gas station, a snow-covered lake with a bridge, streets lined with trees, a train crossing the town, cars parked along the boulevards, people parading by in their holiday best, and even Santa Claus coming to town on his red and gold sled. That's the dream. Here's how we make it come true.

INVITATION

Photocopy and cut out our holiday house. Color it in with crayons or markers and, on the front, write:

CALLING ALL BUILDERS!

FRONT

CONSTRUCTION OF A
HOLIDAY VILLAGE
☆ ☆ ☆ ☆ ☆
begins when you arrive at
5:30 pm on December 19th
at the MURPHY'S
2244 Holiday Lane

INSIDE

R.S.V.P. ☆   555-1234 ☆

2¾"

3½"

FOLD

CUT

1. Place on fold and cut out card house
2. Using x-acto knife cut out 3 sides of the door
3. Add your family members and information. Color.

DECORATIONS

Since your holiday decorations set the stage, all you need is a large table covered with a door-size board. Have several card tables around the room holding the supplies the children will need. In general, you will need the following miniature items that can be found in most hobby and craft shops, and even in some toy stores: trees and plants, moss, dried flowers, cars (you can get bags of wooden, plastic, or metal toy cars at your local toy store), people, train and tracks, holiday decorations, and any other appropriate accessories. Collect small cardboard boxes in all shapes (even cylinders—cardboard tubes from gift-wrapping paper—are good), not forgetting old standbys like mini cereal boxes and shoe boxes (kids' shoe boxes are great because they are small). Arrange on the tables: cement glue, a glue gun, spray glue, paints, straws, markers, lots of scissors, the makings of snow (cotton balls, spray snow, Ivory Snow Flakes™, House Mortar (page 66), mylar paper, glossy blue contact paper, small mirrors, ice-cream sticks, lots of candy, and the like.

❄
You can buy inexpensive plastic construction helmets and give out to your crew. They are sold in most party/stationery stores.

❄
A flat door or a piece of Masonite or plywood or even a plain white plastic tablecloth would do for the work table.

The children will build the houses and bridges for the village and arrange them on the board, then add all those accesories to make the village complete. Remember, the expectation is not to make a museum-quality city but an imaginative creation with everyone's input and ideas.

ACTIVITIES

The main activity is building the village. Begin by laying out the roads and city blocks. Try to plan so each block has enough room for two to three buildings. Houses that are many different sizes make for a more diverse and interesting village, but laying out the streets first will give you a plan from which to work. Now add lots of trees—they come in bags of a dozen or more. The more trees, the better; and the greater the variety, the more real the village will look. Place them along "sidewalks," in front of the houses, along the lake.

The other accessories are up to the kids. You can wrap little matchboxes in pretty paper and place them on each stoop as holiday gifts. You can place buses, trucks, cars, and even traffic signs at various street corners. A park with swings is a possibility, as is a hot dog cart. Miniature animals can be placed here and there or be part of a zoo. Since it is winter, adding snow everywhere is fun to do and beautiful to look at. Instant snowmen can be made out of marshmallows.

Let the children choose the kinds of houses they would like to build. Several children can tackle the one large house together, or they can each make their own. Each child can make a graham cracker house (see Gingerbread House, page 67), a group can make the Sugar Cube "New England" Church (page 68) together, and you can assign different tasks—making bridges, placing trees, decorating the streets—to others. If you have invited more than six children to this party, have them work in groups and/or have them build more than one version of any of the houses.

You can do several things to light the village. Stringing white or colored Christmas lights along the streets and houses creates an instant wonderland.

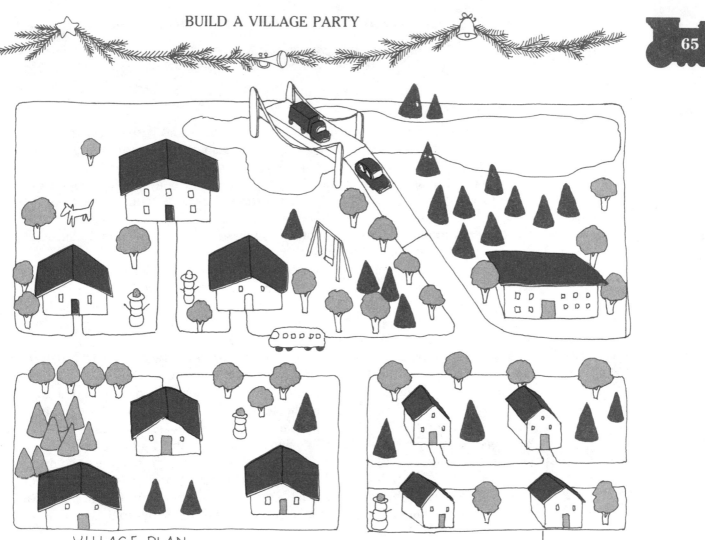

VILLAGE PLAN

You can also place mini flashlights or light sticks (the kind you use at Halloween) inside the houses with windows to let the light shine through.

When the village is done, you can leave it on display at your house for the rest of the holidays or each child can take home the house that he made. Be sure to take instant photographs of each child's handiwork and of the whole village so the kids will have lasting mementos.

❄ Make a log cabin using long pretzel sticks instead of gingerbread.

GINGERBREAD LOG CABIN

Remember the Gingerbread Log Cabin you made in "Deck the Halls" (instructions on page 20)? Be sure to include it in your village plan!

HOUSE MORTAR

2 egg whites
2 teaspoons water
⅛ teaspoon cream of tartar
3 cups powdered sugar

In a mixer, place the egg whites, water, and cream of tartar and beat until just foamy. Add the powdered sugar, 1 cup at a time, and keep beating. When done, you have enough mortar for approximately two shoebox-size houses. For this village party, plan on making this recipe at least four times. For colored mortar, just add food coloring (use as many drops as you need to give you the shade you want).

❄ When making the Candy House, put the heavier candies on a flat roof or they will slide down the sides.

CANDY HOUSE

Building a real gingerbread house takes a lot of time and patience, and the complexity and technique can be overwhelming, particularly for young children. Our friend Bess Armstrong came up with an answer for her son Luke: Since the difficult part of making a gingerbread house is in handling the gingerbread pieces, why not build a gingerbread house without gingerbread? So here is a Candy House, a simple version a child of almost any age can make. It is the perfect centerpiece for the village, a masterpiece that can be the "town hall" in your own magical kingdom.

You can make this house out of any cardboard box (heavier cardboard will hold the candy best). For example, take a shoe box. Remove the top and turn the box upside down. Take the top and make a fold down the middle the long way so you create an instant roof. Glue it to the box (the glue gun will create the strongest bond), and you have an instant house.

Smother the house and roof with House Mortar (left)—the thicker, the better. For variety, you can tint the "mortar" with food coloring so the background of the house is not white. Working quickly before the icing hardens and doing one wall at a time, cover the entire house with candies. Bess uses tiny teddy bear cookies as "tiles" on the roof; mini peppermint sticks, licorice, or pretzels as "logs" on the sides; and M&M's™, small gumdrops, small jelly beans (the big ones may be too heavy), miniature marshmallows, Life Savers, wafers, candy mints, sprinkles, silver balls, Red Hots™, and Gummy Bears™. Shredded coconut makes great snow! You can also make a yard out of aluminum foil and cover a small area with blue icing to make an instant pond. Snowmen out of miniature marshmallows round out the scene.

❊ Make a gingerbread gift by "gluing" graham crackers together with our "House Mortar" to form a box. Let it dry. Now fill with small jelly beans, M&Ms, or Life Savers. Place at each plate for a sit-down dinner, give out as party favors, or use as table decorations.

GINGERBREAD HOUSE

Another popular version of the Gingerbread House is made using graham crackers. It can be made quickly and easily, so if several children make their own at the same time, you'll have a street "instantly" lined with houses.

A milk carton or any other sturdy cardboard box becomes the form for this house. Gather together House Mortar (page 66), graham crackers (use only full pieces, not broken ones), colored icings (either ready-made in tubes, available in the baking section of the supermarket, or colored House Mortar), and assorted candies.

Using the House Mortar as glue, first cover one side of the carton with the icing and place the graham crackers on it. Repeat for the other three sides (to cover the carton). Use as many crackers as you need to cover each side (you may have to slice some in order to fit). The top of the milk carton becomes the roof, or form one with cardboard or the box top if you are using a regular box.

Once all the graham crackers have been "glued" to the box and covered with icing, you can begin to decorate with the candies, forming doors, windows, shutters, and other decorations as you please.

A young child's creation may not look as finished as his older brother's, but he should decorate it as he likes. Windows placed at funny angles won't detract from the masterpiece, since houses come in all shapes, sizes, and colors. Everyone feels like an artist or an architect at the end of this project.

SUGAR CUBE "NEW ENGLAND" CHURCH

You will need three boxes of miniature or regular sugar cubes, House Mortar (page 66) in various colors, colored gel paper, and a small flashlight.

To begin, construct the first side of the church 10 cubes long and 6 cubes high: Place a row of 10 sugar cubes on the table and spread the icing between each cube and across the line of 10 (see drawing below). Press the cubes together tightly so the extra "mortar" oozes out. Wipe the excess with the edge of a plastic knife. Pile another row of 10 sugar cubes for the second row. Place 2 cubes and then leave out 2 cubes for the length of the third row for windows. Repeat this for the fourth row. In the fifth row, you can arch the windows by cutting the closing cubes at a diagonal (see drawing below). Now make the back wall 7 cubes wide by 6 cubes high, no windows. Repeat the side wall. You now have three walls of the church done.

For the front of the church, construct a wall 7 cubes wide and 6 cubes high, allowing a 2-by-4-cube opening for the door. Now, in front of and outside of this wall, you can make a steeple 2 cubes deep, 2 cubes wide, and 11 cubes high. Connect the steeple to the building with your "mortar."

Take some colored cellophane or gel paper and cut out pieces to fit inside the windows of the church. Glue to the inside of the church walls. These "stained glass windows" will give the church a realistic look.

For the roof and the steeple top, use heavy cardboard, preferably in a color. The roof is made from a 7-by-8-inch piece of cardboard, which you fold in half lengthwise. Place it over the church with the sides hanging over the walls (see drawing below). The steeple top is made from three triangles 3 by 3 by 4 inches, taped together. Glue the roof and steeple top to the church with a glue gun.

Place a miniature flashlight inside the church. If you like, you can glue a small brass bell to the top of the steeple.

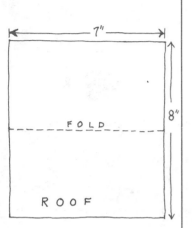

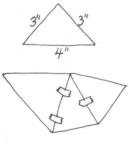

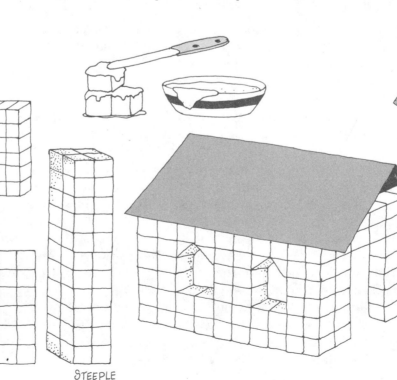

BACK   SIDE

FRONT   STEEPLE

ADD GEL ON INSIDE

HOLIDAY HOUSE

For each house you will need:

1. Cardboard (about a yard square)
2. White Felt (72 inches wide is best):
   Christmas house: approximately ¼ yard green for roof; 1 square (12 inches) red for chimney and door; 1 square (12 inches) yellow for windows
   Hanukkah house: ¼ yard dark blue for roof; ¼ yard light blue for chimney and door; and one square (12 inches) yellow for the windows
3. A miniature wreath or a miniature menorah
4. Two dozen red sequins
5. Pebbles of all sizes for the walkway
6. Homemade Christmas trees or other kinds of trees (see page 17)
7. Rick Rack

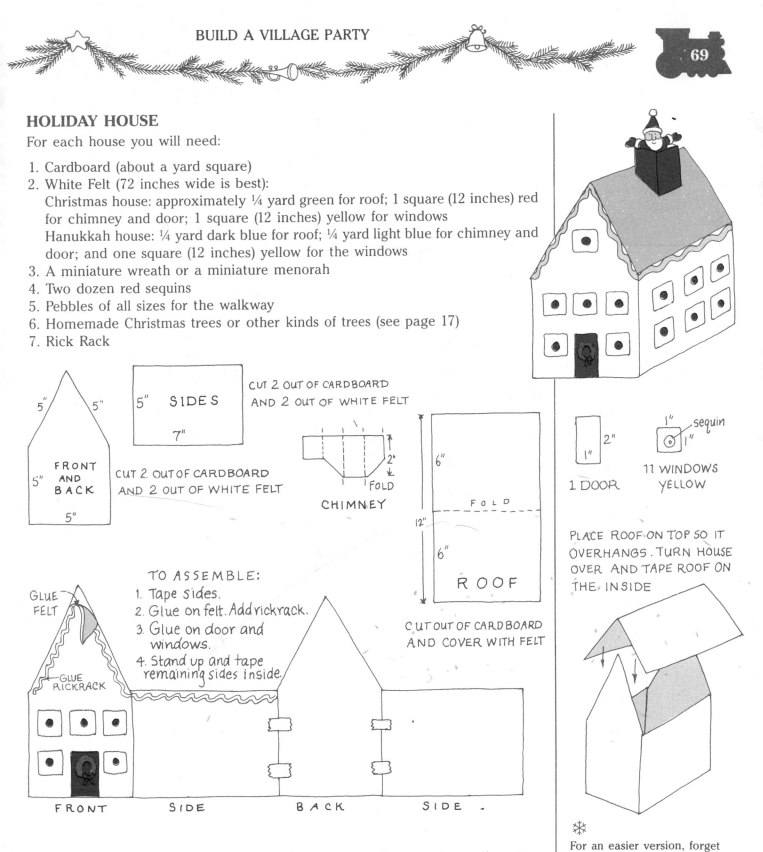

PLACE ROOF ON TOP SO IT OVERHANGS. TURN HOUSE OVER AND TAPE ROOF ON THE INSIDE

❄ For an easier version, forget the felt and make the house out of colored cardboard.

For the finishing touches, glue a wreath or a menorah on the front door. For lights, glue the sequins on the felt windows. You can make a chimney by cutting cardboard squares (see illustration) and taping them together to form a box covered with red or blue felt. (You can have a tiny Santa coming out of the opening). Add a walkway by gluing pebbles leading from the front door. Place a selection of trees in front of the house.

❄
Have some extra marsh-mallows left over from the candy house? Make Marsh-mallow Frosting.

1⅓ cups sugar
½ cup water
6 large marshmallows
3 egg whites
Pinch of salt
1 teaspoon vanilla extract

Boil the sugar and water, but don't stir until the syrup spins a thread. Add the marshmallows; heat until they melt. With an electric mixer, beat the egg whites until they are stiff. Slowly pour the marshmallow mixture into the egg whites while you are beating them. Add the salt and vanilla and you are ready to spread this frosting on any Christmas cookies.

❄
To add people to the village, buy wooden cutouts in the shape of people, paint clothes on them, and glue standing up in the streets. You can also use these, flat, on wrapped gifts.

FAMILIAR LANDMARKS

These are other buildings the children may want to make using their own designs and imagination. They can make a "factory" covered in buttons, a barn with a straw roof, a "supermarket" covered in seashells, a train station, an airport, a water tower, a school, a market, a hospital, a town hall, a band-stand/amphitheater, or a gas station. Encourage the children to use their imaginations to create their own versions of these buildings.

LAKE

You can create a lake on the edge of town in several ways. Get a round or oval mirror and place it on the table board (you can also cut out the shape you want from mylar paper or glossy blue contact paper). Surround your lake with ready-made miniature trees or use evergreen branches, moss, or dried flowers from your yard or flower shop. Put "snow" all around the lake using shaving cream, House Mortar (page 66), Ivory Snow Flakes, or spray snow.

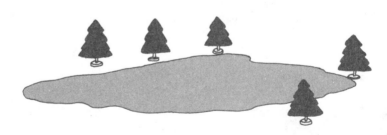

SLEDS

For a real winter village scene, sleds are a must. Use graham crackers and glue on candy canes for the runners with House Mortar (page 66). Place strategically around the lake with tiny people standing by.

MAKING TREES

Rice Krispies™ Christmas Trees

You will find the instructions for making these sensational Christmas trees on page 17. Include them in the village scene; when placed outside a house near the front door, they give the perfect holiday touch.

Nut Trees

Make an 8-inch cone out of heavy cardboard for each tree and staple closed. For ten trees, gather about a pound each of the following nuts in their shells: walnuts, almonds, pecans, filberts, Brazil nuts, and peanuts. Beginning at the bottom of the cone, glue the nuts together tightly to the cardboard, using a glue gun or rubber cement. Vary the nuts so that the tree looks like it's growing different kinds of nuts together. Once you have completely covered the cone in one layer of nuts, add assorted nuts at random to form mounds of nuts on different parts of the tree. You can fill holes between the nuts with the smaller ones and put the others at various angles to give the tree real dimension. When done, you can place these trees together, forming a "nut forest," or spread the different trees you have made all over the village.

Gumdrop Trees

Follow the same instructions as for the Nut Trees (above) but use gumdrops of different sizes to create Gumdrop Trees. These look great in front of the Candy House (page 66), in front of other doorways, or in a cluster for a "Gumdrop Forest."

Christmas Tree Cones

Our friend Obie Slamon taught her young children how to make these when they were four and six, and they have been making them ever since. Simply take sugar cones and place them upside down in muffin tins. Spread green icing over each cone. Now decorate each "tree" by pressing edible candies (Red Hots™, silver balls), tiny gold bells, sequins, or any other decorations into the icing. These become Christmas trees and can be placed at the front doors of the houses. To create simple green trees, don't decorate the cones; these can be placed in clusters to form "forests."

Every year at their Hanukkah party, Jane Rascoff joins sons Justin and Spencer in making "Hanukkah Gelt" trees, which she uses as centerpieces but which would also work perfectly in this village party. Take the same cardboard cone as in the nut tree and glue gold "gelt" (foil covered chocolate coins) all around the tree. You may find it easier to overlap the edges.

※
Should the children get restless toward the end of the party, you can have them play a couple of games. The Hidden Christmas Treasures Game, the Skating Race, or Lights Out in the Tree-Trimming Party (page 41) work well, as well as the Christmas Penny Cat Hunt (page 58).

BRIDGE

Use a cardboard tube from paper towels or wrapping paper, about 1¼ inches in diameter, and cut it in half lengthwise. Now cut a flat piece of cardboard to fit across the open side (also lengthwise) and glue it onto the open side of the tube; this is the pavement part of the bridge. Take four ice-cream sticks and place two at each end and on each side of the bridge, forming the support and suspension towers that will hold the cables. Cut out two pieces of cardboard, 1¼ by 3 inches, and tape one to each end of the bridge, angling down for the ramps. To finish, hang a string from the bottom of the ramp to the top of the closest ice-cream stick and glue, then across the bridge (let it hang down) and glue to the other ice-cream stick at the other end of the bridge, and finally glue it to the bottom of the ramp at the other end (see drawing). Repeat on the other side and the bridge is done. You can glue some tiny cars, trucks, and buses across the bridge. For a last-minute alternative, you can purchase a bridge at a toy store that carries model trains.

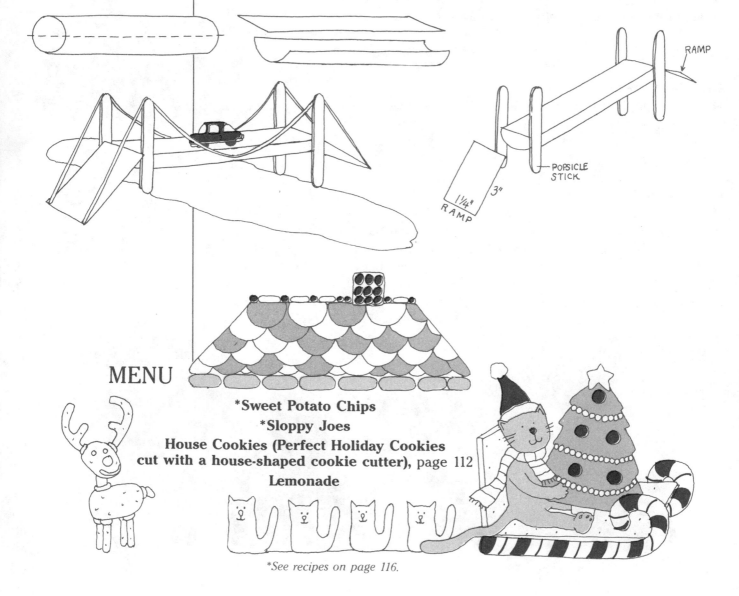

MENU

*Sweet Potato Chips
*Sloppy Joes
House Cookies (Perfect Holiday Cookies
cut with a house-shaped cookie cutter), page 112
Lemonade

*See recipes on page 116.

FAMILY
HOLIDAY
REUNION

73

❄

Your Christmas video will be more interesting if you plan ahead. Remember to have a title, indicate the date (you can zoom in on a calendar or a stocking that has the date on it), and show special things the kids have made. Show a clock face with the early-morning hour if you are shooting the opening of presents on Christmas morning. Be sure to show the Christmas tree with all the gifts under it before they are opened—and then show it after. Show scenes of the kids playing with their new toys, grandparents and relatives arriving for dinner, etc.

Meredith's family has been having family reunions biannually for many years. Their inspiration was her grandfather Guy Harvey, as strong a patriarch figure as you'll ever find. His spirit, the sheer strength of his personality, and the memory of his overwhelming presence with his 300-pound, 6-foot 3-inch frame, capped by a huge Stetson on his head, have remained with the family long after his death. His grandchildren and great-grandchildren, now forty-plus strong, call themselves the "Gramps Gang" and gather for their family reunions to share memories and festivities. Every reunion, they bring new activities to try, lots of pictures to pass around, and stories to tell. One year, in memory of Grandpa Guy, they silk-screened his profile on T-shirts and everyone wore one at the reunion.

In these days, when, more often than not, families are separated geographically, when life is hectic and time seems to fly by at fast forward, it takes real effort to bring families together. And yet, for these same reasons, it is even more important to give our children a sense of family. The holidays, when the spirit of togetherness permeates everything we do, are a great time for sharing the celebrations with your extended family—the kids are off from school, so people have more flexibility with travel—and a family reunion can fit right into the festivities. Whether you celebrate Hanukkah or Christmas (or both), our Family Holiday Reunion jubilee will bring extra joy to your family.

As in all of our parties (but particularly in this one, for it probably includes toddlers and grandparents), we emphasize activities that adults and children of all ages can participate in together. We also suggest that you take some time to gather everyone around the older members of the family and encourage them to share stories of their lives. This works better if the storyteller has some "show and tell" items. Contact this person before the reunion so they can bring scrapbooks, memorabilia, photo albums, or any pieces of clothing that are of particular interest. This party is designed and organized around one day, but if your reunion stretches over a few days, you can spread the activities over that time or you can include activities and ideas from the other parties.

INVITATION

Usually family get-togethers don't require any formal invitation, but sending a copy of an old photograph of the head of the family or a group photo is fun to do. If your child colors in the photocopy with colored pencils, it will look like an antique sepia photograph. You can even send these in flat cardboard frames that the kids make. Somewhere on the photo or at the bottom print the reunion information:

Or you can glue a "head shot" of the head of the family on a cutout of a person from a magazine and photocopy it; that can be very funny.

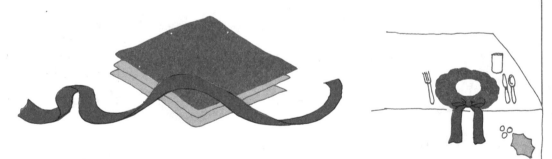

DECORATIONS

If you are planning a sit-down dinner, whether it is one long table for everyone or a couple of tables for children and adults, you and your children can easily make place mats that family members will want to take home with them.

Take 12-by-12-inch felt squares and cut into wreath shapes. Now take soft satin ribbon about 2 inches wide, tie into bows, and attach to the bottom front of each place mat, letting the ribbon hang over the side of the table (see drawing). Have your child write each family member's name on his particular place mat with glitter glue pens. Let them dry overnight.

The rest of the decorations are your family's traditional Christmas or other holiday decorations (celebrants of Hanukkah can have a Hanukkah family reunion).

ACTIVITIES

CHRISTMAS PACKAGE

Divide the crowd into teams. In large garbage bags or cardboard cartons, place the following for each team: all kinds of wrapping paper, bows, ribbons, stickers, tape, scissors, and anything else you can think of for wrapping a package. Now tell each team to select one person to be the Christmas "gift." The object is to have the other members of the team wrap this person as elaborately and unusually as they can. A prize is given for the best "gift," the most imaginative "gift," the funniest "gift," the ugliest "gift," or any other category you can imagine.

FAMILY TREE

Remember those photos you asked each family member to send to you? Collect everyone around a table laden with all kinds of art supplies. You and your child can cut colored ornaments out of construction or wrapping paper. You can also have magazines available so each person can cut out full figures of funny or famous people. Then have everyone glue their photos on the ornaments. Some will be pretty and others, especially those with other figures on them, will be humorous and memorable.

An alternative is to have an instant camera ready and take a photo of each guest as he arrives. These can then be placed on the ornaments. These photos will also help clarify family relationships for the kids—who is related to whom can dictate how the children hang the ornaments on the tree or around the house.

Color code gifts by age. For example, gifts for children under five can be wrapped in green paper, five- to ten-year-olds blue, over ten red.

NAME THROW

Give everyone the paint names you made (see page 17). On the floor, mark out spaces at 2-foot intervals. The object is to throw your name the distance that you call.

WHITE ELEPHANT EXCHANGE

This is an adaptation of Meredith's aunt Lois Gatchell's party game. Each guest brings a "white elephant" gift—something they don't want or need. They sit in a circle, holding the gift during the telling of a story. As the story is told, gifts must be passed to the person on the right or left whenever the words "right" or "left" are mentioned. Speeding up as you go along adds to the fun. The guests keep the gifts they are holding at the end of the story.

The following story can be used as is or can inspire your own version.

The White Elephant Tale

This is a story about Mr. and Mrs. *Wright*. One evening they were baking cookies. Mrs. *Wright* called from the kitchen, "Oh, no, there is no flour *left*! You will need to go to the store."

"I can't believe you forgot to check the pantry," grumbled Mr. *Wright*. "You never get anything *right*!"

"Don't be difficult, dear," replied Mrs. *Wright*. "It will take only twenty minutes if you come *right* back. Go to Fifty-first and Peoria, and turn *left* at the stop sign. Then go to Sixty-first Street and turn *right*, and there it will be on your *left*," declared Mrs. *Wright*.

Mr. *Wright* found the store and asked the clerk where he could find the flour. The clerk pointed and said, "Go to aisle four and turn *left*. The flour and sugar will be on your *left*."

Mr. *Wright* made his purchase and walked *right* out the door. He turned *left*, but he couldn't remember where he had *left* his car. Suddenly he remembered that he had driven Mrs. *Wright*'s car and that his car was in the driveway at home *right* where he had *left* it.

Eventually, a weary Mr. *Wright* found his way home. Mrs. *Wright* had been waiting impatiently. "I thought you would be *right* back," she said. "I *left* all the cookie ingredients out on the kitchen counter, and the cats got into the milk. You'll just have to go *right* out again."

Mr. *Wright* sighed. He had no energy *left*. "I am going *right* to bed," he said. "Anyway, I need to go on a diet, so I might as well start *right* now. Isn't that *right*?"

You can put a picture of your child on the tree. Trace around a cookie cutter on a piece of construction paper and cut out the shape. Stick a face cutout on the shape and hang as an ornament. Or, cut out something from a magazine (a famous person's body or an animal) and place your child's face on that figure, back with construction paper, and hang. These also make great and funny cards.

HOLIDAY DRAW

For this game you will need: 1-by-2-inch slips of paper, an easel (optional), a large pad of white drawing paper, a black felt-tip pen, and an egg timer or a small hourglass.

This is a holiday version of those identification games in which someone has to draw the meaning of a word that he knows but the others don't.

Before the party, write the following holiday-related words, or any others that you come up with, on separate 1-by-2-inch slips of paper. You can also choose words that have particular meaning to your family, words that bring out memories that everyone can recognize and relate to. Print clearly so everyone will be able to read the words. Remember, everyone will have to draw these words, so keep in mind that they should not be too easy, but also include words that very young children know and understand. Here are some suggestions:

manger	merry	reindeer	pancakes
St. Nicholas	dreidel	angelic	fruitcake
popcorn	snow	taffy pull	gingerbread
cranberry	winter	joy	ornament
carol	mistletoe	ringing	evergreen
wrapping	cornucopia		

Separate the guests into two teams—you can have children against adults, or families against families. If your child has an easel he uses for painting, place it in the living room. Attach a large pad of drawing paper and a wide black felt-tip pen. A member of one team picks a word and doesn't let anyone know what it is—not even the people on his team. That person has to draw whatever that word is on the easel and the opposing team has to guess it (use the egg-timer or a small hourglass to define the time constraints). If the opposing team can't guess the word, the person's own team gets a chance. Keep score: The team that guesses the most words wins.

FAMILY ROCK PORTRAITS

Collect smooth stones or rocks (they can be in a variety of sizes but should be round). If you live in the city and have trouble finding them, they are available at most local florists or nurseries. Gather yarn, rhinestones, patches of fabric, eye stickers, and other decorative material. Assign a relative to each child and have the child make his portrait on the rock. These "rock people" can be given out as favors to the adults. You can also choose to have even the adults participate in this, and thus everyone will end up with a rock portrait.

❋
Especially fun for young children: Put out several sets of wooden alphabet blocks and make a game out of spelling as many holiday words as possible.

TAFFY PULL

This is an old-fashioned candy-making process. It takes time and patience and is very good for working your arm muscles!

TAFFY

2 cups sugar
1 cup light molasses
⅓ cup water
2 teaspoons vinegar
2 tablespoons butter or margarine
½ teaspoon baking soda

Butter the sides of a heavy 2-quart saucepan. In it, combine the sugar, molasses, and water. Heat slowly, stirring constantly, until the sugar is dissolved. Then bring to a boil. Add the vinegar and cook to the light-crack stage (268°F on a candy thermometer).

Remove the saucepan from the heat. Add the butter and the baking soda. Stir to mix well. Turn out (don't scrape) onto a buttered platter or a large shallow pan. For even cooling, use a spatula to turn the edges to the center.

Pull the taffy while it is as warm as your hands can handle, using only the fingertips to pull. If the candy sticks, dip your fingers in cornstarch. When the candy is beige in color and gets too hard to pull, cut it in fourths and pull each piece into long strands, about ½ inch thick.

With buttered scissors, quickly snip the taffy into bite-size pieces. Wrap each piece in wax paper.

Makes about 1¼ pounds

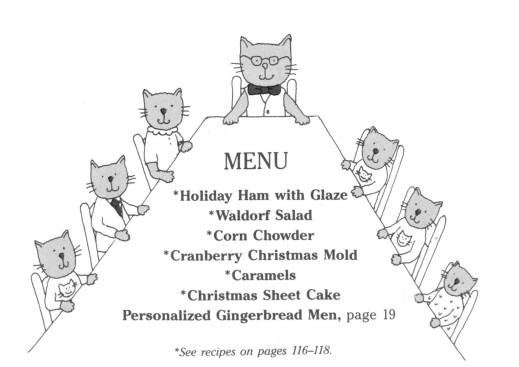

MENU

*Holiday Ham with Glaze
*Waldorf Salad
*Corn Chowder
*Cranberry Christmas Mold
*Caramels
*Christmas Sheet Cake
Personalized Gingerbread Men, page 19

See recipes on pages 116–118.

Pamela Belknap's grandmother polished coins, placed them in a small sack, and gave one sack to each child for Christmas. Sometimes she even found coins with the year of their birth on them, or that year's coins, so they could collect one from each Christmas.

A VERY HAPPY HANUKKAH

The story of Hanukkah, the Festival of Lights or the Feast of Dedication, is the story of miracles, which makes it especially beguiling to children. It is a story that has been told for centuries in Jewish homes all over the world.

Two thousand years ago, the Jewish people lived in Judea. The capital of Judea was Jerusalem, and there, the people built a beautiful temple where they worshiped. The Jews believed in the existence of one God but did not recognize kings, so it meant great trouble for them when, around 336 B.C., Alexander the Great conquered the Persian Empire. Alexander placed

the Jewish people under the rule of Syrian kings, the worst of whom was called Antiochus Epiphanes, who was nicknamed "the mad king" by even those closest to him. He was the cruelest of kings, who told the Jews that he was their god and that they had to bow down to him and worship before him. When the Jews refused, Antiochus destroyed their holy temple, defiled their altars, tore down the holy ark, burned the holy Torah scrolls, and murdered many of the people.

But the Jewish people would not be conquered. A Jewish peasant named Mattathias killed a Syrian soldier who had sacrificed a pig at a Jewish altar (this was sacrilegious in the Jewish religion). Mattathias fled to the mountains with his five sons and formed a guerrilla army. These "Maccabees," as they were called, had no training and no arms, but they vowed to fight their oppressors. They defeated the Syrian soldiers after three long years of fighting and reentered Jerusalem.

When the Jews returned to Jerusalem, they found that their holy temple was ruined. They cleaned the blood off the scrolls and purified the ruined altars. They rebuilt their temple, and on the twenty-fifth day of the month of Kislev (our December), the Maccabees rededicated the temple to the Jewish people. They relit the eternal light using the only holy oil they could find, enough for the light to burn for one day.

But, miracle of miracles, the light burned for eight days and eight nights. And so Jews celebrate this Festival of Lights every year at Hanukkah, the Hebrew word for dedication. Every night for eight nights, while a child or parent recites the Hanukkah blessing, a candle is lit by another candle called the *shammash*, and each successive night an additional candle is lit, until on the eighth night all nine candles of the menorah burn brightly. Families gather together for festive meals, games are played, and gifts are exchanged, one on each night of Hanukkah.

At any time in our history, there are people of many religions and beliefs who are not free to celebrate their holidays. Because Hanukkah celebrates the freedom of people to be who they want to be, and to worship according to their own beliefs, it is especially appropriate to discuss what freedom means to children during the Hanukkah (and Christmas) celebrations.

Sarah Israel makes dreidels from egg cartons. She cuts off two sections of the carton for each dreidel. She paints them and when they are dry, she tapes the open ends together. Sarah then sticks a pencil through the middle of the new "dreidel."

INVITATION

This Hanukkah invitation is a flip book showing the dreidel spinning and spinning until it falls.

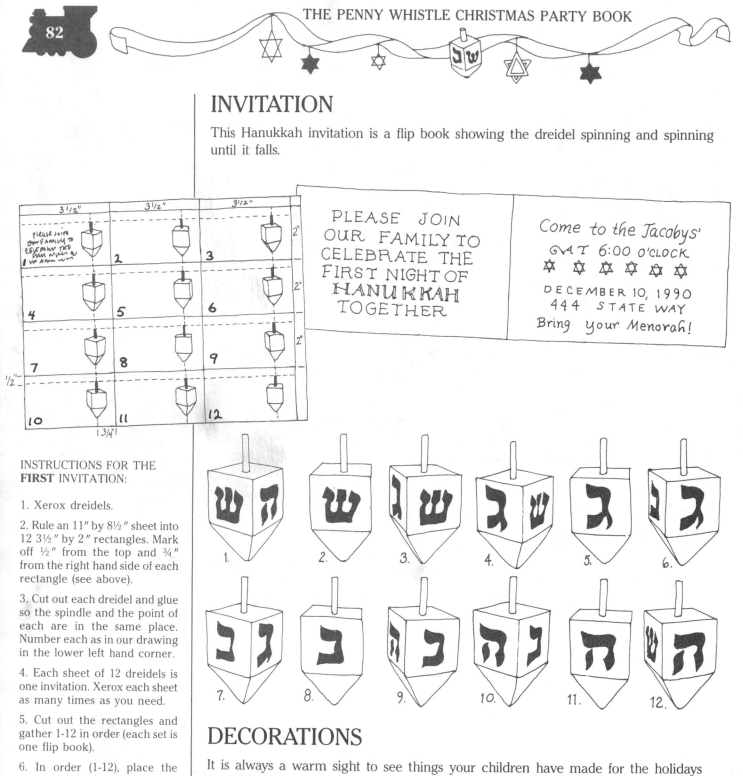

PLEASE JOIN OUR FAMILY TO CELEBRATE THE FIRST NIGHT OF HANUKKAH TOGETHER

Come to the Jacobys' AT 6:00 O'CLOCK ✡ ✡ ✡ ✡ ✡ DECEMBER 10, 1990 444 STATE WAY Bring your Menorah!

INSTRUCTIONS FOR THE **FIRST** INVITATION:

1. Xerox dreidels.

2. Rule an 11″ by 8½″ sheet into 12 3½″ by 2″ rectangles. Mark off ½″ from the top and ¾″ from the right hand side of each rectangle (see above).

3. Cut out each dreidel and glue so the spindle and the point of each are in the same place. Number each as in our drawing in the lower left hand corner.

4. Each sheet of 12 dreidels is one invitation. Xerox each sheet as many times as you need.

5. Cut out the rectangles and gather 1-12 in order (each set is one flip book).

6. In order (1-12), place the pages with each dreidel one on top of the other to form a book (dreidel one is the first page on top). Staple together on the left side and flip! Make all the invitations.

7. Write the "front" invitation copy on the first dreidel page and the "back" invitation copy on the back page of each newly made flip book.

DECORATIONS

It is always a warm sight to see things your children have made for the holidays displayed throughout your home. At Hanukkah, a true family holiday, homemade decorations are especially appropriate and appreciated.

The traditional colors for Hanukkah are blue and white. There are many designs that seem to be popular for this holiday, including anything shaped like a dreidel, the Star of David, and the menorah. Popular holiday foods include doughnuts and pancakes. Any of the decorations can be bought or made and hung around the house. Dreidels look great clustered in baskets on coffee tables. Many of our friends display menorahs they've collected, including the children's annual creations, and those that were received as gifts and bought throughout the years.

ACTIVITIES

GRAB BAG

Everyone brings a gift under a certain dollar amount (for example, under five or ten dollars). Place all the gifts together in a basket decorated with blue ribbons. Place another basket next to it and fill that with slips of paper, each with a number on it (make sure you have the same amount of gifts as numbers). The person who picks number one picks out any gift he wants first. The second person can either pick a gift out of the basket or take the first person's gift. (But, remember, he can't pick one out of the basket, open it, and then decide to take someone else's instead!) If he chooses to take the already-opened gift, the person whose gift he has taken gets to pick another gift. Keep going until all the gifts have been allocated.

For a variation, ask the children to bring one gift for a grab bag and one can of food or a toy. This is part of a tradition that, instead of receiving and giving gifts for the eight nights of Hanukkah, you give a can of food, a gift, or a contribution from your children to those children who are less fortunate.

HANUKKAH TREASURE CHESTS

Dime stores and craft stores carry small plastic boxes in the shape of treasure chests that cost about a dollar. Get one for each child. Collect markers, paints, glitter glue, Hanukkah stickers, small dreidels, and any other small holiday decorations you can find. Each child can decorate his own chest. As the party goes on and each child wins a prize and/or chocolate Hanukkah *gelt* (coins), he can use the Hanukkah chest to store his loot.

Another version of a "treasure chest" for storing goodies is made from the kind of plastic basket that holds strawberries in the market. Gather together thin (¼- to ¾-inch-thick) blue ribbons in all shades and textures. Have each child weave the ribbons through his basket until it is totally covered in ribbons. You can leave the ends hanging and tie blue buttons at each end or just tie them together and cut the ends off. Now cut a bottom out of blue construction paper, place in the bottom of the basket, and you have a blue treasure of a basket!

❄

Jed Schwartz, an animator who also happens to be Jill's brother, was our savior in putting together this flip book invitation. After Jill drew the dreidels, he put the images on his animation computer and helped us make it spin so when you flip the pages, you will see an honest-to-goodness spinning dreidel.

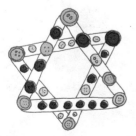

❄

The children can sing "I Have A Little Dreidel" before they play.

SHIN

HE

NUN

GIMEL

DREIDEL GAME

Place either hazelnuts, raisins, jelly beans, chocolate Hanukkah *gelt* (coins), chocolate kisses, or pennies in a pot. Let's say you decide to use pennies. Give each child a dreidel, or use a larger one that all the children can share, and give each child ten pennies. Everyone puts two pennies in the pot. Each dreidel has four Hebrew letters printed on it, one on each side. They are: *nun* for *ness* (miracle), *gimel* for *gadol* (great), *he* for *haya* (happened), and *shin* for *sham* (there). The total of the letters stands for: "A great miracle happened there."

Playing the game: Each child gets to spin the dreidel. If it falls on *nun*, the child takes out nothing from the pot and gives nothing to the pot. If it lands on *gimel*, the child gets the entire pot and everyone puts in two pennies to replenish the pot. If it lands on *he*, the child gets half the pot; and on *shin*, he puts in two pennies. When a child runs out of money he is out of the game. When one child ends up with all the pennies, the game is over and he has won.

To tell you the truth, sometimes this game never ends, so you may want to set a time limit.

STAR OF DAVID

Young children love to make these special stars. Buy a package of ice-cream sticks in a hobby shop or toy store. Using white glue, make a Star of David (see drawing, bottom left). You can decorate the star with paint, or glue with blue or silver glitter, blue buttons, or blue sequins.

Have each child make several. You can hang them at the party or have the children take them home.

EDIBLE DREIDELS

Make these dreidels that the kids can either eat at the party or take home. It is fun to make these together (great for kids three and older). You will need:

Large marshmallows
Chocolate stars or kisses
White frosting
Red licorice
A very thin paintbrush or an eyeliner brush
Blue food coloring

Take each marshmallow and put white frosting on one flat side. Attach a chocolate star or kiss to that side (that will be the bottom of the dreidel). Place them all on a plate and let dry. Cut the licorice into 2-inch lengths.

When all these are assembled, write the appropriate Hebrew letters (see page 84) on the four sides of the marshmallow with the brush and food coloring. Let dry. On the flat side opposite the chocolate candy, stick a piece of licorice in each (it becomes the handle). The kids can eat the dreidels or take them home wrapped in plastic sandwich bags.

HANUKKAH TREASURE HUNT

The clues in this game are set in rhymes and written on small pieces of paper cut in the shape of dreidels. Each clue leads the children to the next clue, with prizes at the end of the trail. The word "Hanukkah" is the starting point—each letter of the word "Hanukkah" is the first letter of an object (read down) that is found in the house (or the party room) and which holds the next clue. Go ahead and use our game below or create your own.

```
H   A   N   U   K   K   A   H
A   P   E   M   E   L   R   A
T   P   C   B   Y   E   M   M
    L   K   R       E   C   P
    E   L   E       N   H   E
        A   L       E   A   R
        C   L       X   I
        E   A       R
```

Keep these words to yourself, as they give away where the clues are hidden.

✳

Barbara and Zev Yaroslavsky (whose edible dreidels appear here) have continued a special Hanukkah tradition in their house. One day out of the eight days, their children, Mina and David, get no gifts. Instead, they either make or buy gifts that they take to their temple to be given to children who are less fortunate.

Divide the children into teams of two or into two teams. Hand CLUE #1 to each team. It reads:

Clue 1

FOR CLUE #2
Here's what you do:
Go to bed and
cover your head.

H

(Clue #2 is in or under a *hat*, which is on the bed.)

Clue 2

FOR CLUE #3:
Here's what you'll see:
One of these a day
Keeps the doctor away.

A

(Clue #3 is under an *apple*.)

Clue 3

FOR CLUE #4:
Walk through a door,
and be sure to check
What fits on your neck.

N

(Clue #4 is in another room and wrapped in a *necklace*.)

Clue 4

FOR CLUE #5:
Don't take a nosedive,
Just walk on ahead
and look under the bed.

U

(Clue #5 is inside an *umbrella* under the bed.)

Clue 5

FOR CLUE #6:
You could be in a fix
So open a door
And you'll see what's in store.

K

(Clue #6 is under a *key* or attached to a key chain hanging from a doorknob.)

Clue 6

FOR CLUE #7:
You may be in heaven
Be sure you don't sneeze
Or you'll need one of these.

K

(Clue #7 is in the *tissue box* in the bathroom.)

Clue 7

FOR CLUE #8:
Do not be late!
To be comfy and fit
March over and sit.

A

(Clue #8 is in or on an *armchair*.)

Clue 8

For the end of the game
Do more of the same
Dirty clothes go in this
And be sure you don't miss.

H

(The hamper is filled with Hanukkah *gelt* or any other prizes.)

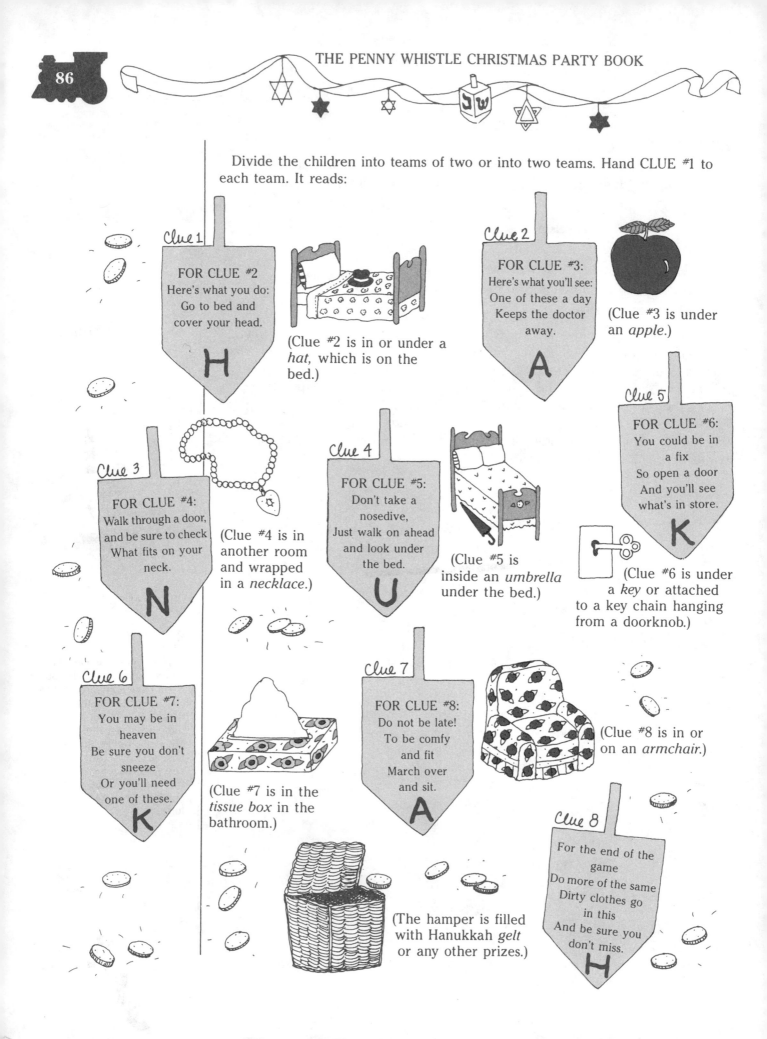

HANUKKAH SONGS

After the games have been played, after the menorahs have been lit and the prayers said (see page 95), that's the perfect time to sit down to dinner and to sing Hanukkah songs. Below are the words to some of the most popular ones.

The magic of candles: Place an assortment on a wide window ledge or in the center of the table for dinner before Christmas or Hanukkah just to get in the holiday mood.

ROCK OF AGES

Rock of ages, let our song,
Praise Thy saving power.
Thou amidst the raging foes,
Wast our sheltering tower.
Furious they assailed us,
And Thine arm availed us.
And Thy word, broke their sword,
when our own strength failed us.

Children of the martyr race,
Whether free or fettered,
Wake the echoes of the songs,
Where ye may be scattered.
Yours the message cheering,
That the time is nearing,
Which will see, all men free,
Tyrants disappearing.

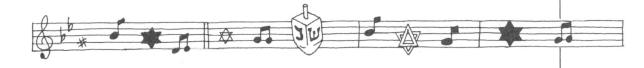

MI-Y'MALEL

Chorus:
Who can retell the things that befell us,
Who can count them?
In every age, a hero or sage
Arose to our aid.
[Repeat]

Hark! In days of yore
In Israel's ancient land,
Brave Maccabees led the faithful band,
But now all Israel must as one arise,
Redeem itself through deed and sacrifice.
(Repeat the chorus)

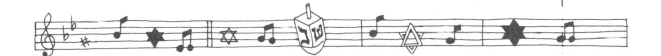

OH! HANUKKAH!

Oh Hanukkah, Oh Hanukkah, come light the menorah,
Let's have a party, we'll all dance the hora,
Gather round the table, we'll give you a treat
Dreidels to play with and latkes to eat.
And while we are playing, the candles are burning low,
One for each night, they shed a sweet light,
To remind us of days long ago,
One for each night, they shed a sweet light
To remind us of days long ago.

I HAVE A LITTLE DREIDEL

I have a little dreidel, I made it out of clay,
And when it's dry and ready, then dreidel I shall play.

Chorus: Oh, dreidel, dreidel, dreidel, I made it out of clay,
Oh, dreidel, dreidel, dreidel, now dreidel I shall play.

It has a lovely body, with legs so short and thin,
And when it is all tired, it drops and then I win!

(Repeat the chorus)

My dreidel's always playful, it loves to dance and spin,
A happy game of dreidel, come play, now let's begin!

(Repeat the chorus)

MENU

*Latkes (Potato Pancakes) with Cinnamon Sour Cream

*Hanukkah Brisket
*Jelly Doughnuts
*Hanukkah Jell-O
*Cheese Pancakes

*See recipes on pages 118–120.

FESTIVAL OF LIGHTS

There are many versions of the menorah, the candelabra that holds the candles that are lit every night of Hanukkah, but every menorah must have eight candles on the same level, and the *shammash*, the candle used to light the other candles, must be higher or lower than the rest. The menorah is traditionally lit at sunset, and the candles are placed from right to left, lit from left to right, and then placed in front of a window.

Making their own menorahs is a wonderful activity for children. Encourage your youngsters to use their imagination and create a menorah of their dreams. And as you save these menorahs and light them throughout the years, your heart will fill with wondrous memories of Hanukkahs past.

INVITATION

This is a cutout menorah with the invitation copy running up and down the candles.

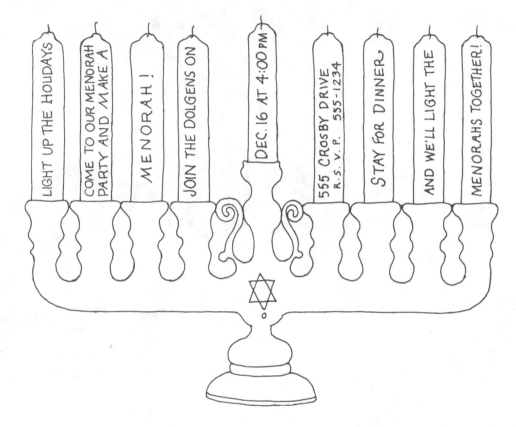

When Avigail Glazer was six years old, she dreamed of having a giant menorah for Hanukkah. She told her mother, Miriam, who took Avigail to their friend Jerry, a furniture builder, who made Avigail's dream come true. Out of wood, boards, and dowels, he created a 5-foot-high menorah that the Glazer family has used for years. Avigail's favorite part of Hanukkah became lighting the "giant" candles (they were really 12-inch-high dinner-size candles) that made other Hanukkah candles puny by comparison!

The invitation candles read: LIGHT UP THE HOLIDAYS · COME TO OUR MENORAH PARTY AND MAKE A · MENORAH! · JOIN THE DOLGENS ON · DEC. 16 AT 4:00 PM · 555 CROSBY DRIVE R.S.V.P. 555-1234 · STAY FOR DINNER · AND WE'LL LIGHT THE · MENORAHS TOGETHER!

DECORATIONS

Menorahs, menorahs, everywhere! You can't have too many menorahs at this party. Besides the Hanukkah decorations we describe in the Very Happy Hanukkah party (see page 82), gather together all the menorahs you have and display them either as the centerpiece in your party room or around the house. Annie collects menorahs and candles and places them all around the house so that in and around the menorahs one is likely to find candles of all shapes and sizes that bring added light. As we call this party for 4:00 P.M., by the time the children have finished making the menorahs, it will be time to light them. Imagine the sight of numerous menorahs and candles bringing a beautiful atmosphere of light to a holiday that reminds us that light is hope!

ACTIVITIES

MAKING MENORAHS

Children of all ages can make any or all of these menorahs. Have the necessary equipment on a large table and let each child choose which menorah he wants to make.

The Thumbprint Menorah

Traditionally, very young children make this menorah out of clay, decorating it with two handprints. David Israel, who is four, has given us these easy instructions for his version, which is a Thumbprint Menorah. First make a menorah base, about 2 by 12 inches, from clay. Using both thumbs, make prints together, with each of nine pairs marking the space for one candle; the candle goes between the two thumbprints. Make a hole before baking. Now bake the menorah following the instructions on the package of clay and you are done.

The Wood and Bolts Menorah

Famous in many Sunday schools, this menorah is simple to make and lasts for years. Moreover, bolts are just the right size to hold Hanukkah candles! The standard one is simple: Glue nine bolts on a flat piece of wood that has been sanded until smooth. Usually, the children paint the wood with brushes, but you can also spray-paint the entire menorah in one color.

Variations of this theme include:

Stacking the bolts one on top of another, making the candles sit higher.

Spraying the wood and the bolts with shiny gold paint.

Using larger bolts and thus larger candles than the traditional Hanukkah candles.

Gluing the bolts in a design instead of in a straight line.

Spray-painting each bolt in a different color paint, placing a variety of colored candles looks in them!

Dipping each bolt in white glue, then dipping it into glitter or silver balls that decorate cakes, then gluing it onto the piece of wood which has also been painted.

Collecting bottle caps, dipping them in different color paints, and gluing them face up on a piece of wood or metal (hardware and lumber stores carry both). Dip the bolts in the paints and let dry. Now place one bolt in each bottle cap, but don't match the colors. The effect will be beautiful!

The Wooden Spool Menorah

At your local fabric or craft store, buy a bag of wooden spools in a variety of sizes. You will need nine each of large, medium, and small sizes, and one extra medium size. These will fit one on top of the other. For a base, you can use a block of wood about 16 by 6 inches, or, as Annie's daughter Lisa did, use an 8-by-10-inch wooden picture frame.

To make the menorah, simply glue the largest spools to the wood using a glue gun. Leave about 1 inch between each spool. Whether you glue them in a row or in the shape of a square doesn't matter, just as long as they are all on the same level. Next, glue a medium spool onto each of the larger ones. Top each stack with a small spool, except for the one in the middle. To this one add another medium-size spool before gluing on the smallest spool; this will be the *shammash.* The result is nine "spool towers." Now, glue a metal bolt to the top of each "tower" to hold the candle.

You can spray each "tower" in a different color paint or all in the same color. You can add designs with glitter, beads, stickers, or any other decorations your child wants to use.

The Clay Menorah

Clay is a magical medium, particularly because it can so easily be shaped in to anything your child imagines. Janet Carnay, a ceramic artist and potter who has been teaching children for twenty years, encourages children of all ages to work with clay. To create yet another original menorah, she suggests buying blocks of clay and having your child make shapes that are inspired by light, for the Festival of Lights. Some suggested inspirations from her young students include clay suns, stars, moons, coils, and the like.

Have your child roll out the clay until it is about ½ inch thick. Then with a star cookie cutter, stamp out clay stars, making ten stars in all. Make a hole with a Hanukkah candle in the center of each star. Bake the stars (following instructions on the package of clay you use) and then place (or glue) them on a platter or wooden block, gluing the extra star on top of the one in the center for the *shammash.* Paint the holders, if you like, and then place a candle in each one.

Other shapes made by using cookie cutters work as well. To make a coil, roll the clay in your hands or with a wooden roller into a pencil shape. Now place it flat on a cutting board and form it into a coil. The center of the coil is the perfect place to put a candle. Repeat the process as with the stars, and the coil menorah is done!

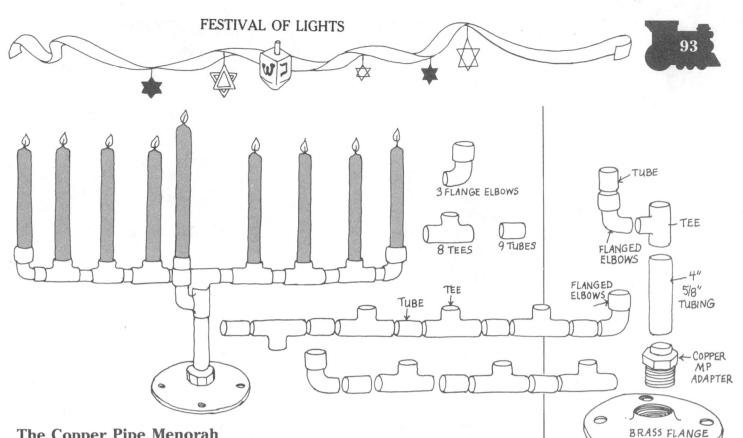

The Copper Pipe Menorah

In any hardware store, you will find a section that displays copper pipes used for plumbing fixtures, which, when assembled together, make wonderful menorahs. Take a list of the items you will need with you and ask an experienced salesperson in the plumbing department for these particular pieces; he will know exactly what you need. The drawing above shows each fitting and how it screws into another. All your child has to do is push each into the next, and a menorah is created in minutes. To make each candle fit, place about an inch square of putty in each hole and push each candle into the putty.

✳ You use forty-four candles in each menorah at Hanukkah!

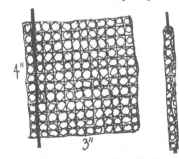

MAKING HANUKKAH CANDLES

For the Festival of Lights, it is a special treat for the children to make their own candles. Here is the easiest and prettiest version.

Buy sheets of beeswax, in white or in colors, and several yards of wicking. Cut the wax into pieces that are 4 by 3 inches (the 4-inch side is the height of the candle). As you work, warm the sheet of beeswax with a hair dryer for about 8 seconds. Place a piece of wicking 4½ inches long along the edge of the length of your candle, letting it extend above the edge of the beeswax sheet about ¼ inch. Using the palms of your hands (kids' hands are the perfect size for this), roll the beeswax sheet away from you. Press lightly to close the edge and you're done! You have made one Hanukkah candle. It takes only a few seconds to make one candle. You can make the forty-four you need for the holiday in no time!

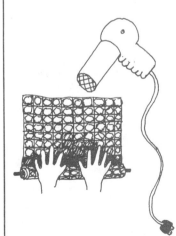

THE MYSTERIOUS MENORAH

Now that the menorahs are made and lit, and before dinner is served (or after, depending on your schedule), the children will be ready to create this mysterious menorah. This is an activity that is especially appropriate and fun for children six and under, although we can name many adults who have been known to get into this creative competition.

Photocopy the drawing of our menorah below. With a pencil, divide the menorahs into the puzzlelike sections, which the children can then color with whatever colors they choose. Encourage them to be creative and to use different colors and even different materials (felt-tip markers, crayons, colored pencils).

When they are done, draw horizontal lines all the way across the menorahs. Turn each piece of paper over and number each strip "inside" the horizontal lines visible from the other side. Have the children then cut the menorahs along these strips. (When done correctly, you will have a number on the other side of each strip.)

Now each child takes his strips and places them on a colored piece of paper. Tape down strip #1 (the top strip). Now take strip #2 and move it slightly to the left of the top strip. Tape that down. Take strip #3 and move it back toward the right, and tape that down. Follow these instructions until all the strips are used up. The result is an abstract menorah that is beautiful enough to frame!

HANUKKAH BLESSINGS

Now that the menorahs and candles are made, it's time to light the candles. Have each child light the menorah he has made.

The children say the following prayers together:

(This blessing, which thanks all the family and friends who have joined together to celebrate the holiday, is said only on the first night of Hanukkah.)

Ba-ruch a-ta a-do-nai
A-lo-hei-nu me-lech ha-o-lam
She-he-che-ya-nu ve-ki-y-ma-nu
Ve-vi-gi-ya-nu laz-man ha-ze.

(This blessing is said over the Hanukkah lights on each of the eight nights.)

Ba-ruch a-ta a-do-nai
E-lo-hay-nu Me-lech ha-o-lam,
A-sher kid-shanu- be-mitz-vo-tav
Ve-tzi-va-nu le-had-lick ner
Shel Hanukkah.

(The next blessing gives thanks for the miracles that saved the Jewish people.)

Ba-ruch a-ta a-do-nai
E-lo-hay-nu Me-lech ha-o-lam,
She-a-sa n-sim le-a-vo-tay-nu
Ba-ya-mim ha-hem ve-ba-zman ha-ze.

At one of Janet Carnay's art classes, an eleven-year-old student, Ronny Buns, took Janet's challenge to create a menorah "in the spirit of light and the intense energy of fire" to heart. Ronny made a 12-inch-high volcano out of clay with a 6-inch hole at the top. He placed the Hanukkah candles in and around the rim of the volcano, and filled the inside with potpourri of cinnamon and cloves.

MENU

*Wild Rice Pancakes
*Zucchini Pancakes
*Apple Sauce
*Noodle Pudding (*Kugel*)
*Challah
Menorah Cookies (Perfect Holiday Cookies cut with a menorah-shaped cookie cutter), page 112

*See recipes on pages 120–121.

NEW YEAR'S NEW COOKS' BRUNCH

The New Year is most often celebrated by adults without children, as they party late into the night on New Year's Eve. Having a New Year's brunch for family and friends not only includes the kids but can give them a central role in the festivities. This party begins with the children cooking the brunch for everyone. All of the items on the menu can actually be prepared and served by the children themselves, but including an adult or two for supervision in the kitchen may not be a bad idea. In addition to the food, there are games and activities that everyone can participate in. Even if watching football is a priority in your house, use some time-outs for a family game or two.

INVITATION

Make a stencil out of the drawing below, replacing it with the numbers of the new year as needed. Photocopy on white or colored paper and cut out for each invitation. Write the copy up and down the numbers.

NEW YEAR'S DAY BRUNCH and THE KIDS ARE COOKING!

JOIN THE SEYMOURS AT 11:00 AM ON JANUARY 1ST.

WATCHING & PLAYING GAMES & WELCOMING THE NEW YEAR! & EATING, COOKING FOR

555 BELL LANE
R.S.V.P. 555-1234

❋ Jerry della Femina and his wife Judy Licht have a "left-over party" for families who have been out of town during the holidays. They serve a variety of holiday dishes to all the friends who missed the festivities the first time around.

DECORATIONS

Buy a plain paper tablecloth for the children to decorate with markers or crayons for the buffet-table cover. (If there are more children than can comfortably fit in the kitchen, this gives them an important project while the food is being readied.) They will very likely have their own ideas, but you can suggest drawing astrological signs or silly forecasts or gluing cutout numbers featuring the new year. Horoscopes from the local paper will attract everyone's attention as well.

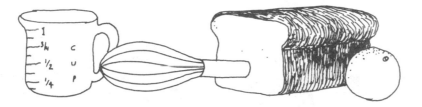

ACTIVITIES

COOKING BRUNCH

The first children to arrive should join your children in the kitchen in order to begin preparing the brunch. All the ingredients, utensils, and equipment should be organized ahead of time and within easy reach.

QUICK TIPS FOR KIDS WHO COOK

- Take your time. Accidents happen when you are in a hurry.

- Wash your hands before you cook, or what's on them will be in your breakfast!

- Wear an apron and shoes. Pull back long hair and roll up your sleeves.

- Read the recipe through before you begin. Make sure you have all the ingredients, utensils, and equipment organized together in one place.

MENU

Because cooking is part of the activities at this party, we have included the recipes for the foods the kids will be making right in this party rather than in the recipe section at the end of the book.

BAKED FRENCH TOAST

Begin making this dish as soon as the first children arrive because it will need to bake for almost an hour.

6 eggs
¾ cup sugar
4 cups milk
¼ cup melted butter
2 teaspoons vanilla extract
¼ teaspoon ground nutmeg
¼ teaspoon ground cinnamon
Pinch of salt
16 slices of French bread with the crusts left on
Powdered sugar
Maple syrup or flavored yogurt, for topping

In a large bowl or a food processor, beat the eggs and sugar for about a minute, until the mixture looks creamy and thick. Add the milk, butter, vanilla, nutmeg, cinnamon, and salt and beat again. Pour into a deep, wide mixing bowl and add the pieces of bread, a couple at a time, pressing them down so they absorb the mixture. Keep adding until the bread is used up, then let stand in the bowl for about 20 minutes.

Preheat the oven to 350°F.

Grease a large glass baking dish. Arrange the bread in the baking dish so the sides overlap one another. Pour the remaining liquid over the bread and bake for about 50 minutes. When done, sift powdered sugar over the entire casserole and serve. You can spoon maple syrup or flavored yogurt over the French toast.

SERVES 8 TO 10

BREAKFAST BANANA SPLIT

1 banana, sliced in half lengthwise
1 cup strawberry yogurt (or any other flavor)
3 tablespoons granola

Place the banana halves on a small plate. Spoon the yogurt on top and sprinkle the granola over the yogurt.

SERVES 1

BLUEBERRY MUFFINS

½ cup butter, at room temperature
1 cup sugar
2 eggs
1 cup sour cream
1 teaspoon vanilla extract
2 cups flour
1 teaspoon baking powder
1 teaspoon baking soda
2 teaspoons ground cinnamon
1 pound blueberries, frozen or fresh

Preheat the oven to 375°F.

In a food processor or with a mixer, cream together the butter and sugar until light and creamy. Add the eggs, one at a time, and continue to mix. Now add the sour cream and vanilla and mix again. In a mixing bowl, sift the flour, baking powder, and baking soda. Add the cinnamon. Add this flour mixture, ½ cup at a time, to the creamed mixture as you continue to beat. When the batter is smooth and creamy, remove into a mixing bowl. Stir in the blueberries using a wooden spoon.

Grease muffin tins or line with paper muffin liners. Fill each tin about three-quarters full. Bake for about 20 minutes or until the tops are brown. When done, let the muffins cool in the tins for about 10 minutes before you remove them.

MAKES 20 MUFFINS

CONFETTI SCRAMBLED EGGS

20 eggs (or 2 per person)
Dash of salt and pepper
5 colors of food coloring: green,
blue, red, orange, and yellow
(yellow is optional, since the eggs
are yellow—but it will give them a
vibrant color)
5 tablespoons margarine

Place the eggs in five small mixing bowls, four eggs in each. Whip each bowlful. Season with salt and pepper. Now add one food coloring to each bowl, using as few as 3 drops or as many as 10, depending on how bright you want the colored eggs to be. The green gets its coloring after 4 to 5 drops; the yellow only needs 2 to 3; red makes the eggs pink, so you won't need more than 5 to 7 drops; the orange and blue look great when they are really bright, so you can use up to 10 drops.

To cook the eggs: Use as many 6-inch frying pans as you have. You will be frying the eggs one color at a time, so the more you pans have, the faster you will be able to cook the eggs.

Melt 1 tablespoon margarine until just foamy. Add the eggs of one color. Using a wooden spoon, move the eggs around in the pan until cooked. Remove to a warm platter and cook the next color. When you are done cooking all the eggs, arrange them on a large serving plate. You can place the colors next to one another or mix them lightly together for a beautiful confetti effect. Serve immediately with toast.

SERVES 10

ORANGE JUICE SURPRISE

2 quarts orange juice
12 strawberries, chopped
1 banana, sliced

Pour half the juice (1 quart) into a food processor or a blender. Add six strawberries and half of the sliced banana. Blend until smooth. Place in a large pitcher and refrigerate. Repeat with the rest of the orange juice, the other six strawberries, and the rest of the sliced banana. Add to the pitcher and serve.

MAKES APPROXIMATELY 10-12 SERVINGS

CINNAMON BACON

2 strips of bacon per person
Ground cinnamon

Preheat the oven to 400°F.
Spread the bacon out on a cookie sheet and bake for 5 minutes. Remove from the oven and sprinkle with cinnamon. Bake for another 5 minutes or until the bacon is crispy.

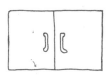

· Be careful of sharp knife blades. Keep them angled away from you when you chop food.

· Once you have used an ingredient, put it back or set it aside. This will make it easier not to forget anything and not to use anything twice.

· Wipe up spills immediately, both on the counter and on the floor.

· Have pot holders handy. Turn pan handles away from the edge of the stove and away from the other burners.

· Be careful when handling dishes from the oven. Always use pot holders and always open lids or foil away from you (so the steam won't blow toward you).

PALM READING

It's always fun for kids to play "fortune-teller." There are many books on palm reading, but here is a simple guide for amateurs that we compiled. Give each child a copy of the palm diagram and accompanying instructions on how to read the future. Then let them loose on the skeptical adults and watch what happens!

Here are some general rules about the lines. Remember:

1. Read all the lines together; the interpretation of one line doesn't mean anything without looking at the whole picture.

2. Every person has a major and a minor hand. If you do everything with your right hand, that is your major hand. In the right-handed person, the left hand tells the story of early childhood and the right hand tells the future.

3. Any forks (or little lines) coming out of the main lines always indicate greater power. Thus, a fork at the end of the life line means good health and great activity until the end of your life. A fork on the head line means greater mental power. A fork on the heart line means a strong heart and a caring for friendship and love.

4. If the hand has many little lines going in all directions off the main lines, you are a person who worries about everything. Having only a few little lines means you are a calm person.

The color of the lines is also significant:

· Very pale or white lines mean poor circulation.
· Very red lines indicate a full-blooded person who may not like heat.
· Yellow lines mean reserve and pride.
· Dark brown lines indicate an emotional person who doesn't forgive easily.
· Pink lines mean cheerfulness and optimism.
· Wide, dark lines indicate a quick-tempered, passionate person who is not easily controlled.
· Pale, wide lines mean uncertain health.

A guide to the lines follows:

1. The Life Line—This line tells the story of your health, your level of activity, and your accomplishments. A long life line means a long life; a broken life line means something in your early life changed your life (the death of a loved one, a marriage, a move to another place, etc). If the life line goes straight down, you will stay close to home throughout your life. If the line curves widely, you will have a life full of activities in many places. If the life line goes across the palm and ends to the left of the center, it means a very successful life. If it curves around the base of the thumb, it means you are very emotional.

2. The Head Line—This line tells how well adjusted you are. If it is deeply curved, you are impulsive and affectionate. If it twists and turns, you can't make up your mind. If it lies low on your hand, you are cheerful and optimistic. If it lies near the heart line, it means your head usually rules your heart.

If you have a Ouija board, it's a great time to get it out and find out what the future holds.

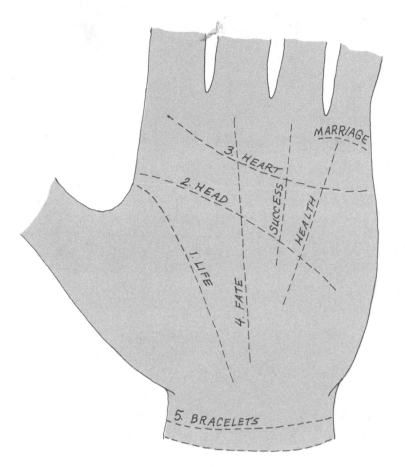

Fill a bowl with fortune cookies so everyone can pick out fortunes all morning long.

3. The Heart Line—This line rules your emotions. If it is well defined, you have strong, deep, and loyal affections, and a big heart. If it is broken in many places, you have been disappointed in love. If it looks like it has chains around it, it means you like to flirt. If it is thin and pale, you love yourself a lot. If it has many lines crossing it, you have had (or will have) many loves.

4. The Fate Line—This is also called the line of destiny. Not everyone seems to have a fate line. If you don't have one, it means luck, chance, or fate play no part in your life (or you are the master of your own fate). If it is a clear and well-developed line, you will have great success. This line usually tells about success, failure, tragedy, and changes over which you have no control. If this line twists and turns, you are supersensitive and this could interfere with success. If it has some parallel lines running with it, your success is being interfered with by outside influences. If it branches out at the beginning, you have had good luck early in your life. If it breaks at the heart line, then you have had sad friendships and love affairs. If it is very deep, long, and straight, you have great luck in money matters. If it is faint but easily seen, you have good success but you worry about it.

5. The Bracelet—This is formed by the two lines found at the top of your wrist. If the bracelet is perfectly straight across the wrist, you have excellent control of your nerves. If it curves up, you are nervous.

SPORTS WORD SEARCH

Created by Marc Gilbar, who is the consummate sportsman in the Gilbar household, this puzzle hides words having to do with various sports. Find the words listed below in this puzzle:

```
H I K E S D V G W I O P L K N G P A S S G F D L L A B B F G R T Y E L O I K H L P O A J G
W I N J H G O H U M B Y C E N T E R Y T U R L O K I J U H G T F R D A H J D C E R T D H U
T O L Y E N D R U N D O N T S O T T L O F O O T B A L L K T R Y L Z T Y T L I S A T C L A
O N L I M P O S A C K V Z X C S F R J A Q W N B L D E R C V G A R Y E T A C K L E U B F R
U N G L I Y E L L C H E E R R A H R A F R T K I C K O F F G O T E A R U N A N N I E D R D
O F F S I D E D P M M B I G T E N G B E S C U B F D G W P O M P O M A M A R C J H F U I P
X Q U A R T E R B A C K F E I F R V D T O Y R F T D E R N T I M D E L G T V C X J N H Y Q
F T B L L E N A G I H C I M I N T E R Y A R D X N T E N K P L A N K R D G H I T Y D V I M
S A C G R N O G I E L F G O A L S C A R T Y G B U F S C B A H E L M E T L J K H I C X R W
C S R P M D F B H F U I T Y G N J G Y T L A N E P H I K Y N G R A A L T R D E R B E R D Y
```

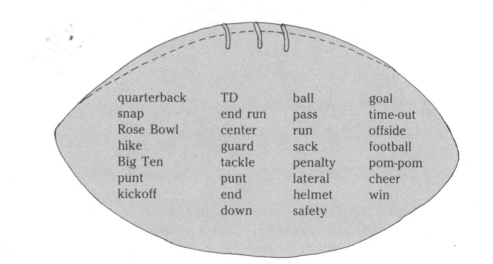

quarterback	TD	ball	goal
snap	end run	pass	time-out
Rose Bowl	center	run	offside
hike	guard	sack	football
Big Ten	tackle	penalty	pom-pom
punt	punt	lateral	cheer
kickoff	end	helmet	win
	down	safety	

MAKE NEW YEAR'S RESOLUTIONS

Copy this New Year's Resolution certificate so that you have one for each guest. Write each guest's name on a small piece of paper and place it in a bowl or a hat. Hand out the certificates. Have each guest draw a name out of the "hat" and keep that name a secret. The object is for each person to write out a resolution for the person he picked, and give it as a gift to that person.

❄

Bea Surmi carries on a tradition she learned from her mother in Budapest, Hungary. On New Year's morning, the children wash their hands in the kitchen sink with a silver dollar; it is thought to bring prosperity in the New Year.

MY NEW 1992 YEAR'S RESOLUTION is to _____

"HORSE" BASKETBALL

As a relief from football and a chance to get some exercise, play this version of that old game "horse" that has been a standard on city sand lots and in high school gyms all over the country, but be sure to use a foam rubber basketball, the indoor variety. First, hang a basketball hoop on the top of a door frame. Divide the guests into teams (you can pit the children against the adults or mix ages and families together). The object of this game is to force the opposite team to become the "horse" by missing more shots than your team. It's played like this:

A player on the first team chooses a spot from which he wants to shoot. (He wants to get the shot in, so he chooses a spot he is comfortable shooting from, but, at the same time, he doesn't want his opponent, who will be shooting from the same spot, to get his shot in, so choosing the spot is a careful game of strategy in itself!) He shoots, and when he makes the basket, a player on the other team must duplicate the shot with one try (from the same spot). If he gets the ball in as well, his team is spared an *h*. If he misses, his team has the first letter, *h*. As soon as team #1 misses, team #2 sets up the next throw to be duplicated. The game progresses until one team spells the word "horse" and loses.

Remember: The strategy is to try to make your own shot difficult so it will be harder for the other team to get their shot.

❄

As last-minute fill-ins, play the games you received as gifts during the holidays!

CATCH A WORD

Everyone gets to play this game in turn. The first person has to say a *two-word* word or phrase. For example, he says, "Good-bye." The next person has to choose one of those words and combine it with another to form yet another *two-word* word or phrase. Thus the second player could say, "Good luck." The third player could say, "Bad luck." The fourth could then say, "Bad boy," and so on.

TWELFTH NIGHT

January 6, the Twelfth Night after Christmas, has long been an important date on the Christian calendar. That is the night that the Three Wise Men, having traveled twelve days since spotting the bright star in the eastern sky, reached Bethlehem and gave their gifts to the Christ child. But this holiday, which has been widely celebrated for hundreds of years in many countries, incorporates many customs that are not religious in origin. Taking down the Christmas tree, packing away ornaments, and serving dinner to family and friends (including a traditional cake that hides a bean or a tiny doll—whoever gets the hidden treasure becomes king or queen for the day) are just some of the rites that have been associated with Twelfth Night. Legend also has it that failure to take down the Christmas decorations on Twelfth Night may mean bad luck for the rest of the year. And in Italy, it is on Twelfth Night, called the *Epifania*, that a witch fills the children's stockings with toys and sweets if they were good, and with coal if they were bad.

The celebration of Twelfth Night, once a popular ritual, has seemed to fade over the last century. But there are some good reasons to keep the tradition alive. With today's hectic pace, it seems fitting to make an event out of the "closing of the season." Children who have been looking forward to the holiday season all year will appreciate the opportunity to have a ceremony of taking down the tree and packing away ornaments and decorations. At the same time, it is the perfect excuse to gather neighbors and close friends who have been away over Christmas. This version of Twelfth Night is a party that combines all of the above, plus adds some games and activities for all to enjoy.

INVITATION

For each invitation, cut two stars—one 6 inches and one 5 inches—out of colored tagboard (gold or silver looks great). Glue the smaller star to the larger one, or glue a small (1-inch-square) piece of foam rubber or sponge between the two to make a three-dimensional invitation. Outline a smaller star in white paper; write the invitation information with a black felt-tip marker and photocopy enough copies for each invitation. Cut out each star and glue on each invitation.

❇
Bess Armstrong's mother, Louise, never remembered to take the prices off the children's Christmas ornaments and decorations. Since she always bought them at the end of the holiday season at great savings, the children always thought that Santa was a pretty thrifty fellow.

GLUE ON SPONGE
GLUE TO SPONGE

TWELFTH ☆ NIGHT
JANUARY 6TH
6:00 PM - 8:00 PM
at the Murphy's
555 Park Lane
All the Wise Men Are Coming
HOPE YOU ARE TOO!
R.S.V.P.   555-1234

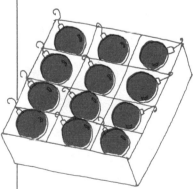

ACTIVITIES

You can put your guests to work taking down the tree and decorations, and packing up the ornaments for next year, or you can all enjoy the tree and decorations for one last evening. Either way, everyone will want to participate in any or all of the following games and activities.

THE TWELVE DAYS OF CHRISTMAS

The "Twelve Days of Christmas" is the perfect song to sing with your entire crowd. Copy these words so that every guest has his own sheet. Divide the guests into twelve groups. You can do this in several ways—children under five, those between five and ten, adults over a certain age, or moms, dads, friends from across the street, those from this side of the street and so on. Assign one of the twelve days to each group, and then sing in turn.

In Mary Slawson's hometown of Portland, Oregon, the custom was to end the holiday season by having all the neighbors gather their Christmas trees in one spot and light a bonfire. Remembers Mary, "It was a wonderful way to bring the season to a true close."

On the first day of Christmas, my true love gave to me,
A partridge in a pear tree.

On the second day of Christmas, my true love gave to me,
Two turtledoves (repeat gifts in descending order).

On the third day of Christmas, my true love gave to me,
Three French hens (repeat).

On the fourth day of Christmas, my true love gave to me,
Four calling birds (repeat).

On the fifth day of Christmas, my true love gave to me,
Five golden rings (repeat).

On the sixth day of Christmas, my true love gave to me,
Six geese a-laying (repeat).

On the seventh day of Christmas, my true love gave to me,
Seven swans a-swimming (repeat).

On the eighth day of Christmas, my true love gave to me,
Eight maids a-milking (repeat).

On the ninth day of Christmas, my true love gave to me,
Nine pipers piping (repeat).

On the tenth day of Christmas, my true love gave to me,
Ten drummers drumming (repeat).

On the eleventh day of Christmas, my true love gave to me,
Eleven lords a-leaping (repeat).

On the twelfth day of Christmas, my true love gave to me,
Twelve ladies dancing (repeat).

TWELFTH NIGHT THEATER

This party is the perfect setting for your children to perform a play that they've written. The kids create the characters and action, but you might want an older child or an adult to act as the director. The idea is to create a play that will be fun for the kids to perform. They don't have to memorize lines but rather will enjoy performing extemporaneously.

For story ideas, let your child look through his own bookshelf and choose some favorite stories to act out (it is helpful to do this before the party so you can be prepared with appropriate costumes and props). Some books we recommend include *Willy Wonka and the Chocolate Factory, Caps for Sale*, and the *Madeleine* books. A tape recorder with a selection of tapes for suitable accompaniment is also a great touch.

Set aside a special room in the house where the kids can rehearse. Organize the props and any costumes the kids might need so that when they are ready to rehearse, they can prepare without any adults. While they are rehearsing, you can arrange chairs together in one place, facing a "stage." You can also:

• Suggest that the children create a "Playbill" for their performance, complete with a cast of characters and other credits, to be handed out to the audience.

• Get real tickets (available in stationery stores), which lend credibility to the children's efforts.

• Have the kids make popcorn and serve it in small paper bags.

• Assign someone to be the "lighting director" and have him hold the flashlight as a spotlight. You can also cover the flashlight with gel paper in different colors to create colored spotlights.

CHRISTMAS CHALLENGE

Copy the puzzle so that each guest gets a copy. Divide the guests into two or more teams. The first team to guess all the answers wins. The answers to our puzzle are as follows:

1. Snowfall
2. Reindeer
3. Halo
4. Holiday
5. Taffy Pull
6. Advent
7. Happy New Year
8. Holy Night
9. *The Night before Christmas*
10. "All through the house"
11. "Silent Night"
12. "Dashing through the snow"

❄ Mistletoe, holly berries, and poinsettias are toxic and should be kept away from small children, who are likely to put them in their mouths.

AND THE ANSWER IS...

In celebrating the coming new year on Twelfth Night, it is fun to predict what the future will hold. If you're lucky, "Three Wise Men" will come to your party to prognosticate the future or scrutinize the holidays.

The game is played by giving answers and guessing the questions. For each turn, three guests get to be the "Wise Men." Provide either turbans or crowns (paper crowns are available at party shops) for them to wear and have them sit apart from the other guests. Place cards, each with a question on one side and the answer on the other, in a hat. A guest picks a card and reads the answer. Each "Wise Man" has a chance to come up with the question. When they finish guessing, the guest reads the answer. When the "Three Wise Men" have finished, three other guests might be chosen to fill those roles.

Here are some sample answers and questions:

1. The answer is: "Snow White"; the question is: "What is the real color of Aunt Mary's hair?"

2. The answer is: "Mistletoe"; the question is: "What do you call an armed foot?"

3. The answer is: "Three Wise Men"; the question is: "What would you never call Larry, Moe, and Curly?"

4. The answer is: "Silent Night"; the question is: "What do you call Sir Lancelot with his mouth full?"

5. The answer is: "Lift-off"; the question is: "What is Santa's command to his reindeer?"

You get the idea. And the funnier, more outrageous, and personally meaningful the answers, the better. You'll soon be able to come up with questions that relate to your family and your life. We're betting your children will probably come up with the best questions!

※

Meredith and Tom are avid bird watchers. One way they get to see some of the most beautiful birds in the northeast is by making bird feeders and hanging them outside their home. Here's how you can make your own: Collect large pine cones. With a small plastic knife, spread peanut butter on as much of the surface as you can cover. Roll the entire cone in birdseed. Hang in a tree outdoors.

COLLAGE CREATIONS

Instead of throwing out your old Christmas cards this year, collect them in a pile and have the children make a giant collage. They can cut out figures and place them on construction paper and include their own photos, small ornaments, and leftover ribbons and wrapping paper.

Instant stickers: Buy contact paper appropriate for your gift-wrapping theme. Cut out your own abstract designs, or draw or trace holiday shapes from cookie cutters and then cut out. Remove the backing and stick on the package.

MENU

The menu at this party includes foods that are simple to make and simple to eat. We have collected more recipes than you may want to use, but a table full of finger foods offers a good selection and people will appreciate the choice.

*Miniature Chili-Cheese Turnovers
*Super Nachos with Sausage
*Refried Bean Dip
* Taquitos
*Guacamole
*Twelfth Night Bombe
*King Cake

*See recipes on pages 121–124.

THE PARTY RECIPES

❄ You don't have to clean cookie sheets between baking. Just remove the pieces of cookie, make sure the sheet is still greased, place more dough on it, and use again.

❄ To paint a cookie: Add ½ teaspoon powdered sugar to one egg yolk. Divide into three bowls. Add 8 to 10 drops of food coloring. Using a small watercolor brush, paint the designs on the frosted cookies, taking care to clean the brush between colors so they won't mix.

❄ Store cookies in airtight containers. When ready to serve, place them on a cookie sheet and pop in the oven just before serving. Bake for 2 minutes to make them fresh again.

SANTA'S WORKSHOP

PERFECT HOLIDAY COOKIES

½ cup butter, at room temperature
1 cup sugar
2 cups sifted all-purpose flour
¼ teaspoon salt
½ teaspoon baking soda
1 large egg, beaten
1 tablespoon milk
1 teaspoon vanilla extract

With a mixer or in a food processor, cream together the butter and sugar. Sift together the dry ingredients; add to the butter mixture and beat well. Add the egg, milk, and vanilla and beat again until well mixed. Shape the dough into two balls, wrap in wax paper, and refrigerate for at least 1 hour.

Preheat the oven to 350°F.

On a floured board, roll out the dough until it is ⅛ inch thick (the thinner, the better). Cut into shapes with cookie cutters and place 1 to 2 inches apart on baking sheets.

Bake for about 10 minutes. The cookies should not get brown! Cool on racks.

ICING

1 cup powdered sugar
1 egg white
Food coloring of your choice

With an electric mixer, mix the powdered sugar and egg white. Divide into small bowls and tint each with food coloring (the number of drops of food coloring depends on how strong you like the color—the more drops, the stronger and darker the color). You can now spread the frosting onto the cookies with a flat knife or pipe it.

MAKES ABOUT 3 DOZEN COOKIES

CRANAPPLE PUNCH

1 gallon cranberry-apple juice
½ cup sugar
¼ cup lemon juice
1 cup orange juice
1 quart bottle seltzer (or to taste)

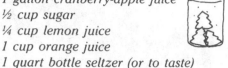

Place the first four ingredients in a punch bowl and let sit for a few hours. When ready to serve, add the seltzer and ice. For an added treat, make colored ice by freezing water and food coloring in ice trays of holiday shapes.

TREE-TRIMMING PARTY

OYSTER STEW

Meredith makes this Oyster Stew every Christmas Eve.

5 tablespoons butter
1½ pints shucked oysters and their liquid
1 cup milk
2 cups cream or half-and-half
Salt and freshly ground pepper
Cayenne
Chopped parsley

Heat soup bowls and add a pat of butter to each bowl. Drain the oysters, reserving the liquid, then heat the milk, cream, and oyster liquid to the boiling point. Add the oysters and bring again to a boil.

Season to taste with salt, pepper, and cayenne. Ladle into the hot bowls and add a sprinkling of chopped parsley.

SERVES 4–6 ADULTS

WASSAIL

2 lemons, peeled and juiced
3 oranges, peeled and juiced
6 cups water
1½ cups sugar
1 to 2 sticks cinnamon
1 tablespoon whole allspice
Rinds of oranges and lemons
1 gallon apple cider

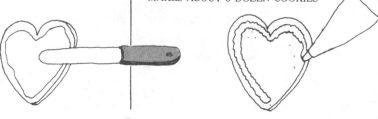

Combine the lemon and orange juices and set aside. In a saucepan, heat the water and sugar. After the sugar dissolves, add a stick or two of cinnamon, the whole allspice, and the rinds of the oranges and lemons, then simmer for 1 hour.

Refrigerate until ready to serve. When ready to use, add the apple cider and the lemon and orange juice. Heat until hot but not boiling. Serve in mugs with individual sticks of cinnamon.

APPROXIMATELY 6 QUARTS

CHRISTMAS CRUDITÉS

Arrange cleaned, cut-up red, green and white vegetables on a large platter. Red and green peppers, cherry tomatoes, snow peas, string beans, broccoli, cauliflower, mushrooms and jicama are all good choices.

YULE LOG

Our friend Ellen Wright suggests running a fork over the frosting to make it look more like a log.

> ½ cup flour
> ½ cup unsweetened cocoa
> 1 teaspoon baking powder
> ¼ teaspoon salt
> 4 eggs, separated
> ¾ cup sugar
> 1 teaspoon vanilla extract
> ¼ to ½ cup raspberry jam
> Chocolate Butter Frosting
>   (recipe follows)

Preheat the oven to 350°F. Generously butter the bottom of a jelly roll pan. Line with wax paper and grease again.

Combine the flour, cocoa, baking powder, and salt. Set aside.

Beat the egg whites until foamy. Gradually add half of the sugar to the egg whites, beating constantly until they form stiff peaks, and set aside.

In a large bowl, beat the egg yolks until thick and lemon-colored. Add the rest of the sugar plus the vanilla; beat until very thick. Add 2 tablespoons water. Now, gradually add the flour mixture, folding into the egg yolk mixture after each addition. Gently fold in the beaten egg whites.

Spread the batter in the prepared cake pan. Bake for 18 to 22 minutes or until the cake springs back when lightly touched. Loosen the edges; immediately turn onto a towel. Starting at the narrow end, roll up the cake in the towel. Cool.

When the cake is cool, remove the towel. Spread the cake with raspberry jam or the chocolate frosting and roll up again. Frost the top with Chocolate Butter Frosting. Decorate.

CHOCOLATE BUTTER FROSTING

This can be used both inside and outside the Yule Log.

> 4 tablespoons butter, at room
>   temperature
> 2 cups powdered sugar
> 1 teaspoon vanilla extract
> 2 squares unsweetened chocolate,
>   melted, or ½ cup unsweetened
>   cocoa

In a mixer, cream the butter and sugar well. Add the vanilla and chocolate until totally mixed and spreadable.

SMOKED TURKEY ON A STICK

> 25 slices smoked turkey
> Margarine
> Mustard
> Mayonnaise
> 25 thick breadsticks

Spread each slice of turkey with margarine, mustard, and mayonnaise. Roll one slice around each breadstick and dab with a little margarine to seal the edges. Arrange on a platter and serve.

25 STICKS

❄

To make blue sugar for decorating, simply place a few tablespoons of sugar in a glass bowl and add blue food coloring, 1 drop at a time, until the sugar becomes the shade of blue that you want.

❄

Susan Russell's family in San Antonio holds an annual Christmas cookie exchange. They invite ten to twelve other families, and each family brings two dozen of their favorite cookies. They spread them out on a table and each family chooses cookies to take home.

When making frosting, whether for decorating or for holding candies and cookies together, you may have to adjust the ingredient amounts. For example, with two large eggs, you may need slightly more powdered sugar. Or if your eggs are small, you may have to add an additional egg white.

Cut gumdrops into shapes such as flower petals, stems, and the like, dipping the shears in hot water between cuts. Stick to sugar cookies with frosting.

I'M DREAMING OF A WHITE CHRISTMAS

ICE-CREAM PIES WITH CRUSHED PEPPERMINT

Pack softened vanilla ice cream into individual tinfoil pie pans and freeze. When ready to serve, let stand at room temperature a few minutes, then unmold. Crush candy canes in a food processor and sprinkle over the ice-cream pies.

COCONUT SNOWBALL

½ cup butter, at room temperature
1½ cups sugar
4 eggs
2 cups unbleached all-purpose flour
2½ teaspoons baking powder
½ teaspoon salt
¾ cup milk
1 teaspoon vanilla extract
Grated rind of 2 oranges
White Frosting (recipe follows)
4 cups sweetened flaked coconut

Preheat the oven to 325°F. Grease a 10-inch bundt pan.

Cream the butter and sugar together in a mixing bowl until light and fluffy. Add the eggs, one at a time, beating well after each addition.

Sift the flour, baking powder, and salt together. Add to the creamed mixture, alternating with the milk. Mix well after each addition.

Fold in the vanilla and grated orange rind. Pour the batter into the prepared bundt pan.

Bake for 50 to 60 minutes or until the edges shrink away slightly from the sides of the pan and a knife inserted into the center comes out clean. Let the cake cool in the pan for 30 minutes before turning it out onto a cake rack.

When the cake has cooled, cover the hole with a cardboard circle. Frost the entire cake, making sure not to move the cardboard. Sprinkle with the coconut.

WHITE FROSTING

1½ cups sugar
1 teaspoon cream of tartar
4 egg whites
½ cup cold water
2 tablespoons vanilla extract

In the top of a double boiler, cook the sugar, cream of tartar, egg whites, and water. When combined, remove into a bowl and beat with an electric mixer until the frosting looks like well-beaten egg whites (this should take between 5 and 7 minutes). Continue beating until the frosting stands and peaks. Now beat in the vanilla.

SNOW PUDDING

This is Sue O'Halloran's family's favorite dessert.

1 tablespoon unflavored gelatin
¼ cup cold water
1 cup boiling water
1 cup sugar
¼ cup lemon juice
3 large egg whites

Soak the gelatin in the cold water and then dissolve in the boiling water. Add the sugar and lemon juice. Strain and set aside in a cool place. Occasionally stir the mixture and when thick enough (stick a spoon in it and if the pudding stays on the spoon, that's enough), beat with a wire whisk until frothy.

With an electric mixer, beat the egg whites until stiff enough to hold their shape. Fold the egg whites into the gelatin mixture. Put into a mold or into small bowls. You can also serve it cold with Soft Custard (recipe follows).

ENOUGH FOR 6–8 ADULTS

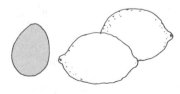

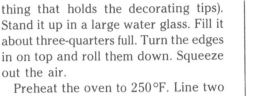
SOFT CUSTARD

3 egg yolks plus 1 whole egg
¼ cup brown sugar
⅛ teaspoon salt
2 cups scalded milk
½ teaspoon vanilla extract

Beat the eggs slightly with a fork. Add the sugar and salt. Add the milk gradually, stirring constantly. Cook and stir in a double boiler over hot but not boiling water until the mixture coats a spoon (it should take about 7 minutes). Strain. Add the vanilla and chill.

MERINGUE MUSHROOMS

This is not complicated or difficult, even though it may sound like it. When you've done it once, you'll be so excited by the results, you'll make them many times. Kids love to whip the egg whites, flatten them with wet fingers, and put them together with the chocolate. It's a wonderful family project.

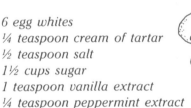

6 egg whites
¼ teaspoon cream of tartar
½ teaspoon salt
1½ cups sugar
1 teaspoon vanilla extract
¼ teaspoon peppermint extract
1 tablespoon unsweetened cocoa
1 12 ounce bag semisweet
  chocolate chips

With an electric mixer, beat the egg whites until they are foamy. Gradually add the cream of tartar, salt, and sugar, and then add vanilla and peppermint extracts. Beat until stiff and then beat some more, so when you turn the bowl upside down, nothing moves. This will take you at least 10 minutes—don't panic if it's more like 15 or even 20.

Fit a large (18-inch) pastry bag with the inside part of a standard coupler (the thing that holds the decorating tips). Stand it up in a large water glass. Fill it about three-quarters full. Turn the edges in on top and roll them down. Squeeze out the air.

Preheat the oven to 250°F. Line two cookie sheets with brown paper or parchment paper.

Make the stems. (You do the stems first because the meringue will be stiffer at this point and you need the stems to be stiff in order to hold the caps.) Squeeze out the mixture 1½ to 2 inches high by pulling up on the pastry bag. You can place the stems very close together because if they stick they will come apart easily later.

For the caps, push down on the pastry bag instead of pulling up—this will form the caps easily. When done, wet your forefinger and push down on the little squiggly that forms on the top of each cap. Keep wetting your finger every five caps or so.

Take a sifter or a mini strainer and put the cocoa powder in it (a little at a time). Sprinkle over the caps and stems and then blow it off the cookie sheets. This creates an airbrush effect on the mushrooms, giving them a touch of color.

Bake for a least 1½ hours. The meringues are done when they lift off the paper easily. Turn off the oven and leave the meringue pieces in the oven to cool as the oven cools. Take them out and cut off the tip on top of each stem.

Melt the chocolate chips in the microwave or in the top of a double boiler.

Take a small knife and put a dab of chocolate on the bottom of each cap and press it gently on the top of a stem. Let the chocolate set up by putting them upside down in egg cartons or muffin tins. When dry, they can be put out on trays, or individually wrapped as gifts.

MAKES ABOUT 4 DOZEN MUSHROOMS

❄ Jill's Meringue Mushrooms make great gifts. Put them in berry boxes from the market and wrap in colored cellophane.

❄ You can string these with gold thread and hang on the tree.

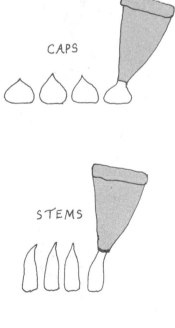

CAPS

STEMS

pat down tip

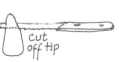
cut off tip

Frost bottom of mushroom cap with chocolate

Stick the cap and stem together

❄ Sprigs of holly are a beautiful Christmas ham garnish. They are also great for decorating packages.

CHRISTMAS DIVINITY

1½ cups sugar
½ cup water
2 tablespoons light corn syrup
⅛ teaspoon salt
One 7-ounce jar marshmallow cream
1½ teaspoons vanilla extract
1 cup chopped pecans

In a large saucepan, combine the sugar, water, corn syrup, and salt. Cook over medium to high heat to the hard-ball stage (250°F on a candy thermometer). Place the marshmallow cream in a large mixing bowl. Beat, gradually adding the syrup mixture to the marshmallow cream. Beat until stiff and the mixture forms peaks. Now beat in the vanilla and pecans. Quickly drop by heaping teaspoonfuls onto wax paper. Store in an airtight container.

MAKES ABOUT 2 DOZEN CANDIES

BUILD A VILLAGE

SWEET POTATO CHIPS

Heat 3 inches of vegetable oil in a wok to 375°F. Peel sweet potatoes and slice them on a slicer or in a food processor to the desired thickness. Fry until crisp. Drain on paper towels.

Season with salt, or for a more interesting taste (says our friend and caterer Don Ernstein of Wonderful Foods in Los Angeles), season with super-fine sugar and cinnamon.

SLOPPY JOES

2 tablespoons butter
¾ cup minced onion
½ cup chopped green pepper
2 pounds lean ground beef
1 teaspoon sugar
4 tablespoons chili sauce
12 sandwich buns

In a saucepan, melt the butter and sauté the onion and green pepper until translucent. Add the ground beef. Cook until the meat is lightly browned. Add the sugar and chili sauce. Simmer, uncovered, over low heat for 15 minutes. Toast the sandwich buns and fill with the meat mixture.

MAKES 12 SANDWICHES

FAMILY HOLIDAY REUNION

HOLIDAY HAM

This is Nora Ephron's favorite recipe, served at her family Christmas dinners.

One 14 to 15 pound precooked ham (with bone)
1 box whole cloves
One 10-ounce jar apricot jam

Preheat the oven to 325°F.

Place the ham in a roasting pan and bake for 3 hours. Remove from the oven and score the fat in a diamond pattern, cutting only ¼-inch deep. Stud with the whole cloves.

Empty the jar of apricot jam into a saucepan and warm over low heat. It will become runny. Rub through a strainer and smear over the ham. Raise the oven temperature to 450°F and bake for ½ hour, spooning the glaze over the ham two or three more times.

This ham is perfect for a buffet table. It tastes as good at room temperature as it does right out of the oven and will serve twenty people for a main course, more if many of them are children or if you're serving other entrées.

SERVES AT LEAST 20

WALDORF SALAD

2 cups peeled and diced tart apples
1 tablespoon sugar
½ teaspoon lemon juice
Dash of salt
1 cup 1-inch julienne celery sticks
¼ cup broken California walnuts
¼ cup mayonnaise
½ cup whipping cream, whipped

Sprinkle the apple cubes with the sugar, lemon juice, and salt. Add the celery and nuts.

Fold the mayonnaise into the whipped cream. Gently fold into the apple mixture. Chill. Serve in a lettuce-lined bowl.

Note: You can add 1 cup halved seedless grapes to the above.

SERVES 6

CORN CHOWDER

4 tablespoons unsalted butter
1 cup peeled and diced potato
1½ cloves garlic, minced
1 cup chopped onion
1 cup chopped celery
4 cups fresh raw corn (or two 10-ounce
  packages frozen)
4 cups chicken stock
4 cups milk
¾ cup chopped parsley
1½ teaspoons salt
¼ teaspoon pepper

Melt the butter in a saucepan and sauté the potato, garlic, onion, and celery until tender, about 10 to 15 minutes. Add the corn and cook another 6 minutes.

Add the chicken stock, milk, parsley, salt, and pepper. Bring to a boil, then reduce the heat and simmer for 10 minutes. Serve piping hot.

SERVES 8

CRANBERRY CHRISTMAS MOLD

Make this the day before the party.

1 pound cranberries
2 cups orange juice
½ cup honey
2 tablespoons unflavored gelatin
Grated rind of 1 orange
1 can mixed fruit or fruit cocktail,
  drained
1 cup chopped walnuts (optional)
½ pint heavy cream, whipped until it
  holds soft peaks
1 Jell-O mold in the shape of a star
  or Christmas tree

Boil the cranberries in the orange juice. When the berries have popped, add the honey and gelatin. Let the mixture cool. Fold in the orange rind, canned fruit, nuts, and whipped cream. Pour the mixture into the mold. Refrigerate until set.

When ready to unmold, slide a knife around the edge of the mold to loosen the sides. Dip the mold in warm water in the sink for 5 seconds. Put a serving platter or tray on top of the mold and turn upside down.

CARAMELS

1 can Eagle™ brand sweetened
  condensed milk
½ pound melted butter
2 cups brown sugar
½ cup Karo light syrup
Pecans, finely chopped

Mix the first four ingredients and heat gently over medium heat for ½ hour, stirring constantly. Continue cooking over medium heat for 1 hour more, until it reaches between 230° and 235°F on a candy thermometer. You may need to lower the heat to prevent burning.

Pour the mixture over the pecans in an 8-by-8-inch buttered pan or stir in the nuts before pouring. Refrigerate until firm. Cut into squares and wrap the individual pieces in plastic wrap.

MAKES 3 DOZEN

❄ Dollypops: For younger children, stick toothpicks (points off) in gumdrops, dip quickly in milk, and roll in powdered sugar.

❄

For a variation on potato latkes, use sweet potatoes (boil until just tender). Add 1 teaspoon vanilla, 1 tablespoon ground cinnamon, and 1 teaspoon ground nutmeg. Leave out the onion, salt, and pepper. Proceed with rest of recipe.

❄

If you prepare the brisket 1 to 2 days ahead of time, refrigerate covered in aluminum foil. Then, when you are ready to serve it, slice the cold meat (it's easier to slice the meat when it is cold) and put the slices, tightly packed together (along with any gravy), back into the aluminum foil. Heat in a 325°F oven for about 10 minutes.

CHRISTMAS SHEET CAKE

2½ cups all-purpose flour
1½ cups sugar
1 teaspoon salt
3 teaspoons baking powder
1¼ cups milk
⅔ cup safflower oil
2 eggs plus 2 egg yolks
2 teaspoons vanilla extract
Buttercream Frosting (recipe follows)

Preheat the oven to 350°F. Grease and flour a 9-by-13-inch or an 11-by-15-inch baking pan.

In a large bowl, mix together the flour, sugar, salt, and baking powder. In a food processor, using the steel blade, blend the milk and oil. Add the flour mixture and blend well for about 2 minutes. Now add the eggs and vanilla and blend again until the batter is very smooth, about 2 minutes.

Pour the batter into the baking pan. Bake for 40 to 50 minutes or until a knife inserted in the middle of the cake comes out clean. Let it cool for at least 1 hour before frosting.

When cool, cut with a sharp knife into the shape of a Christmas tree. Frost with green Buttercream Frosting. Place a candle at the tip of each tree "branch."

Note: An electric mixer may be used in place of a food processor.

BUTTERCREAM FROSTING

1 cup butter, at room temperature
½ cup milk
½ teaspoon salt
2 teaspoons vanilla extract
2 pounds powdered sugar

Put the butter, milk, salt, and vanilla in a large mixing bowl. Cover with about 3 cups powdered sugar. Beat until smooth and creamy. Add the remaining sugar, a little more or less depending on how thick you want the frosting. This can be colored and spread with a spatula or used in a decorating bag.

A VERY HAPPY HANUKKAH

LATKES (POTATO PANCAKES) WITH CINNAMON SOUR CREAM

Annie's Mom, Esther Ancoli Barbasch, never peels the potatoes in this, her recipe, because, she says, "It's tastier, healthier, and easier!"

6 potatoes
1 small onion, chopped
Dash of salt and pepper
2 eggs
Flour
½ cup vegetable oil
Cinnamon Sour Cream (recipe follows)

Grate the potatoes. If they are very watery, let stand for a few minutes after grating and pour off or spoon off the excess water. Mix them with the onion, salt, and pepper. Add the eggs. Add enough flour to absorb the extra moisture.

Heat the oil in a skillet (there should be about ¼ inch in the pan) until it is very hot. Drop the batter by soup spoonfuls and fry until brown. Turn only once and fry on the other side. Remove to a platter covered with paper towels to soak up the excess oil. Serve with Cinnamon Sour Cream.

MAKES ABOUT 20 PANCAKES

CINNAMON SOUR CREAM

2 cups sour cream
½ teaspoon ground cinnamon
½ teaspoon sugar

For 2 cups of sour cream, blend in ½ teaspoon ground cinnamon and ½ teaspoon sugar. Spoon over each pancake.

HANUKKAH BRISKET

Another tidbit from Esther, "I've made brisket every way possible, and the favorite still seems to be the simplest. So don't be fooled by how easy this is to make. It is delicious!"

Two 4-pound front-cut briskets
2 packages Lipton's Onion Soup Mix

Preheat the oven to 350°F.

In a roasting pan, place the brisket in a large piece of foil. Sprinkle the soup over the brisket. Cover the brisket completely with foil, leaving air between the meat and the foil but folding the foil so tightly that no air can escape. Bake for 2 hours. Transfer to a serving platter and slice thinly across the grain.

SERVES 16

JELLY DOUGHNUTS

Annie's sister, Dr. Sonia Ancoli-Israel, makes these with the kids all year round, figuring that they shouldn't be saved just for the holidays.

1 package active dry yeast
¼ cup warm water
1¾ cups scalded milk
½ cup butter
¾ cup sugar
1 teaspoon salt
Dash of nutmeg
Grated rind of ½ lemon
1 egg or 2 egg yolks
6 cups flour
Preserves of your choice
Egg whites
¼ cup powdered sugar

Dissolve the yeast in the warm water. To the scalded milk, add the butter, sugar, salt, nutmeg, and lemon rind. When lukewarm, add one beaten egg or two beaten egg yolks. Stir in the yeast and only enough flour to make a soft dough. Knead the dough until smooth and elastic. Cover tightly with plastic wrap and let rise until doubled in bulk.

Roll the dough ½ inch thick on a lightly floured surface and cut into rounds with a biscuit cutter. Place a teaspoon of preserves in the center half of the rounds. Brush the edges with egg white and cover with plain rounds. Press the edges to seal.

Place on a well-floured surface and let rise until very light. Heat 3 to 4 inches of oil to a temperature of 360°F. Fry a few doughnuts at a time, turning once, until brown. When done, the doughnuts will have a white strip around the center. Drain on crumpled paper towels. Sprinkle with powdered sugar.

HANUKKAH JELL-O

Betty Brown's children are known as the "Jell-O lady's" kids because her holiday Jell-O mold is such a favorite. It's a treat for the kids to make with Mom the day before the party, and the results impress everybody! Here is our version:

Two 6-ounce packages
   raspberry Jell-O
One 6-ounce package lime Jell-O
½ cup sour cream
One 3½-ounce package lemon Jell-O
Pineapple spears or rings
Cherry halves
Jellied cranberry sauce
Miniature marshmallows

Make the first layer: Prepare the raspberry Jell-O according to the mold directions on the box. Put it aside to cool. When partially set, pour into a 9-by-13-inch glass pan. Refrigerate until firmly set.

Make the second layer: Prepare the lime Jell-O according to the mold directions on the box and put it aside to cool. When partially set, beat in the sour cream. Don't blend totally because it looks pretty with small flecks of green and white mixed together. Pour on top of the raspberry layer. Return to the refrigerator until set.

Make the third layer: Prepare the lemon Jell-O according to the mold directions on the box. Cool until the gelatin is partially set. Remove the pan with the two gelatin layers in it from the refrigerator and pour the lemon Jell-O over the lime layer. Now, working quickly, arrange the pineapple spears,

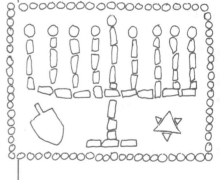

flat, to form the shape of a menorah. Place a cherry half on top of each "candle." Cut the jellied cranberry sauce into dreidel shapes and lay flat on either side of the menorah. Outline the entire mold with miniature marshmallows. Refrigerate until serving time. Place on your serving table and cut into squares when ready to serve.

CHEESE PANCAKES

2 eggs
1 to 2 tablespoons sugar
2 cups small curd cottage cheese
1 cup sifted flour (can use more if needed)
½ teaspoon salt
½ teaspoon baking powder
1 cup oil for frying

Separate the eggs. Beat the yolks with the sugar. Add the cottage cheese and flour, salt, and baking powder. Beat the egg whites until they hold soft peaks, and fold into the cottage cheese mixture.

In a frying pan, heat oil to a depth of one inch until hot. Drop the mixture by the tablespoonful into the oil. Flatten with a spatula and brown, one side at a time, turning only once. Drain on paper towels and garnish with sour cream or jam.

FESTIVAL OF LIGHTS

WILD RICE PANCAKES

This is our friend Karen Emmer's popular variation on the traditional potato pancake for Hanukkah. They have become such a holiday favorite that Karen's kids insist they help their mother make them all year round.

1 bunch scallions, white and green parts minced
1 tablespoon butter or margarine
1 cup wild rice, rinsed
1 cup water (more if needed)
1 cup flour
1 teaspoon baking powder
3 eggs
1¼ cup chicken broth
Salt and pepper to taste
2 tablespoons oil, for frying

Sauté the scallions in the butter until soft. Add the rice and water. Bring to a boil, cover, and simmer for 45 minutes or until the rice is tender. Add more liquid as necessary. Drain off any excess liquid and cool.

In a mixing bowl, combine the flour and baking powder. In another small bowl, beat together the eggs and broth and stir into the rice. Combine with the flour mixture and season to taste with salt and pepper.

Heat the griddle and coat with the oil. Using a ⅓-cup measure, ladle the batter onto the griddle and turn only once, when the underside is brown. Finish cooking on the other side and remove to a cookie sheet. You can warm these up as necessary in a toaster oven.

ZUCCHINI PANCAKES

2 pounds zucchini, grated and drained
3 to 4 eggs, slightly beaten
½ teaspoon baking powder
¼ to ½ cup matzo meal
1 tablespoon sugar
Salt and pepper to taste
1 cup oil

Mix all the ingredients together except the oil, adding enough matzo meal to make the batter thick.

Heat oil in a frying pan until hot. Spoon a tablespoon of the batter onto the pan and cook until the underside is brown. Turn only once and brown the other side. Drain on paper towels and serve.

APPLE SAUCE

8 to 10 baking apples, cored, peeled, and quartered
2 tablespoons fresh lemon juice
½ teaspoon ground cinnamon
1 tablespoon honey

Place the apples in a crockpot. Add the other ingredients and cook on low for about 8 hours.

NOODLE PUDDING (*KUGEL*)

Ruth Hirschhorn's noodle *kugel* is famous on the East Coast, and her grandchildren have been reluctant to share this recipe, until now.

1 pound medium flat egg noodles, cooked and drained
6 eggs
1 cup sugar; 5 tablespoons reserved
½ pound melted butter; 5 tablespoons reserved
1 pint sour cream
¾ pound (1½ large packages) cream cheese
1 tablespoon lemon juice
1 teaspoon grated lemon rind
2 cups corn flakes

Grease a 9-by-12-inch glass baking dish.

In a large mixing bowl, combine the noodles, eggs, sugar (except 5 tablespoons), butter (except 5 tablespoons), sour cream, cream cheese, lemon juice, and lemon rind. Place in the baking dish and refrigerate for 1 hour (or overnight).

Preheat the oven to 350°F.

When ready to bake, combine the corn flakes with the reserved 5 tablespoons each of sugar and butter and sprinkle this mixture over the cold kugel. Bake for 1½ hours and serve hot.

CHALLAH

4½ to 5½ cups unbleached flour
1½ teaspoons salt
1 package active dry yeast
⅓ cup margarine
1 cup very warm tap water
4 eggs, at room temperature
⅓ cup honey
1 teaspoon cold water
¼ teaspoon poppy seeds (optional)

Preheat the oven to 350°F.

Mix 1¼ cups flour with the salt and yeast. Add the margarine and warm water and beat with an electric mixer for 2 minutes. Add 3 eggs and the white of the fourth, reserving the yolk for the glaze. Add another ½ cup flour and the honey. Beat at high speed for 2 minutes.

Stir in the rest of the flour 1 cup at a time. The dough will be sticky. Knead 8 to 10 minutes and put in a greased bowl. Let rise, covered, for 1½ to 2 hours or until doubled in bulk.

Punch the dough down. Divide in half. Now divide each half in thirds. Roll into ropes and braid three strands. Repeat with the other half. Place in lightly greased pans. Let rise for another 1½ hours. Paint with the egg yolk mixed in the cold water. Sprinkle with the poppy seeds. Bake for 25 to 30 minutes.

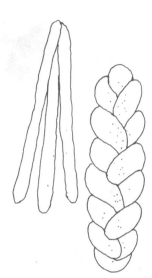

❋
Adrienne Horwitch adds yellow raisins while kneading.

TWELFTH NIGHT

MINIATURE CHILI– CHEESE TURNOVERS

1 package pie crust mix (enough for a double-crust, 9-inch pie)
2¼ cups (9 ounces) shredded sharp Cheddar cheese
2 egg whites, lightly beaten
1 4-ounce can California green chilies, seeded and cut into 1-inch squares

Preheat the oven to 400°F.

Prepare the pie crust mix according to the package, adding water as directed. Stir in 2 cups of cheese.

Divide the pastry in half. On a lightly floured board, roll out one half of the pastry to ¹⁄₁₆-inch thickness. Using a cookie cutter or the top of a glass, cut into 2½-inch rounds. Moisten the edge of each round with egg white; place a piece of chili and about ¼ teaspoon of the remaining cheese in the center of

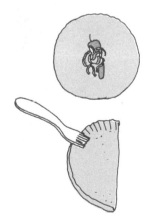

each. Fold in half, press the edges together with a fork, and place on lightly greased baking sheets. Repeat the procedure with the remaining half of the pastry.

To serve, brush with egg white and bake, uncovered, for about 12 minutes (14 minutes if frozen) or until lightly browned.

Note: These turnovers may be prepared ahead of time, refrigerating them, covered, overnight or, for longer storage, wrapping them tightly and freezing until ready to bake.

MAKES 3½ DOZEN

SUPER NACHOS WITH SAUSAGE

½ pound each lean ground beef and chorizo sausage, casing removed, or 1 pound lean ground beef
1 large onion, chopped
Salt
Tabasco sauce
One or two 16-ounce cans refried beans
1 4-ounce can whole California green chilies, chopped (for milder flavor, remove seeds and pith)
2 to 3 cups shredded Monterey Jack or mild Cheddar cheese
¾ cup prepared taco sauce (green or red)
Garnishes
8 cups corn-flavored tortilla chips

GARNISHES:
¼ cup chopped green onion (including tops)
1 cup pitted ripe olives
8 ounces avocado dip (or 1 medium-size ripe avocado, peeled, pitted, and coarsely mashed) topped with sour cream
1 mild red pickled-pepper
Fresh coriander (cilantro)
Fresh parsley sprigs

Preheat the oven to 400°F.

In a frying pan, crumble the ground beef and sausage. Add the onion and cook on high heat, stirring until the meat is lightly browned. Drain the fat. Season with salt and liquid hot pepper seasoning to taste.

Spread the beans in a shallow 10-by-15-inch oval or rectangular pan or oven-proof dish. Cover evenly with the meat. Sprinkle the chilies over the bean and meat mixture, cover evenly with the cheese, and drizzle with the taco sauce. If making ahead of time, cover and chill. Bake, uncovered, for 20 to 25 minutes or until very hot throughout.

Remove from the oven and quickly garnish with some or all of the toppings.

Tuck the corn-flavored tortilla chips around the edges of the bean mixture, making a festive border. Serve at once.

The bean mixture can be scooped up with the tortilla chips, if desired. Set the platter hot on an electric warming tray while serving.

MAKES 10 TO 12 APPETIZER SERVINGS

REFRIED BEAN DIP

This dip is perfect for a large party.

2 cups refried beans
1 cup shredded Cheddar cheese
½ cup chopped scallions with some tops
¼ teaspoon salt
2 to 3 tablespoons taco sauce
Tortilla chips

In a heatproof dish, mix together the refried beans, cheese, scallions, salt, and taco sauce. Cook, uncovered, over low heat, stirring until thoroughly heated. Garnish the top with a handful of cheese and some onion. Warm over a candle warmer. Serve with tortilla chips for dipping.

MAKES 3 CUPS

TAQUITOS

For one cheese taquito:

Roll one or two slices of cheddar cheese in a soft corn tortilla. Hold the rolled tortilla with tongs and deep fry in 2 inches of hot oil for 2-3 minutes; the tortilla should be crisp and the cheese melted.

For beef or chicken taquitos:

Roll 2-3 thin strips of sautéed chicken or beef in a soft corn tortilla. Deep fry as above; the tortilla should be crisp and the meat heated through.

Note: Be sure to hold the tongs with a potholder, as they will get very hot.

GUACAMOLE

4 ripe avocados, mashed
½ cup sour cream
1 to 2 drops Tabasco sauce
1 garlic clove, minced
½ teaspoon salt
¼ cup fresh lemon juice
4 ounces Cheddar cheese, grated
4 ounces Monterey Jack cheese, grated
4 medium tomatoes, diced
½ cup chopped green onions
½ cup sliced pitted black olives
¾ cup sour cream
1 cup salsa
Tortilla chips

Combine the avocados with the ½ cup sour cream, Tabasco, garlic, salt, and lemon juice. On a serving platter, layer the ingredients in the following order: avocado mixture, cheeses, tomatoes, green onions, olives, sour cream, and salsa. Serve with tortilla chips.

SERVES 8

TWELFTH NIGHT BOMBE

This is a refreshing end to this Mexican feast.

2 quarts raspberry sherbet
2 quarts lime sherbet

Line a 2-quart Pyrex bowl with plastic wrap. Soften 1 quart of the raspberry sherbet and place a layer 2 inches thick in the bowl. Freeze for half an hour. Spoon 1 quart of softened lime sherbet on top of the raspberry and freeze for another half hour. Now add the rest of the raspberry and freeze again. Repeat with the rest of the lime. When finished, freeze overnight.

To serve, turn the bombe over onto a platter (it will come right out of the mold). Arrange sliced lemons and limes around the base of the bombe.

Optional raspberry sauce: Puree a bag of frozen raspberries in a food processor. Add ½ cup sugar or more to taste; strain and spoon over each serving of the bombe.

KING CAKE

This recipe makes two cakes, which will serve about twenty-six people.

1 package active dry yeast
1 plus ½ teaspoon sugar
¼ cup lukewarm water
1 teaspoon salt
1 cup butter, at room temperature
1 cup scalded milk
3 eggs
½ teaspoon vanilla extract
½ teaspoon lemon extract
¼ teaspoon mace
4 cups sifted all-purpose flour
⅓ cup chopped pecans
Two 1-inch dolls (for the surprise!)

Topping:
1 cup powdered sugar
1 teaspoon vanilla extract
Water
¾ cup sugar
Green, yellow, and blue food coloring

Dissolve the yeast and 1 teaspoon sugar in the lukewarm water. Set aside. In a large mixing bowl, combine the rest of the sugar, the salt, ¼ cup butter, and the milk. Beat with an electric mixer on low speed until well blended. Cool until lukewarm.

Beat 2 eggs. Add the yeast mixture, vanilla, lemon extract, mace, and 3 cups flour. Mix until smooth. Stir in the re-

maining flour, a little bit at a time. When the mixture has the consistency of dough, keep it in the same bowl and cover with a damp towel. Let rise in a warm place until doubled in size or for about 1½ hours.

On a lightly floured board, roll out the dough into the shape of a square about 1 inch thick. Dot with half of the remaining butter and fold in half. Repeat the process. Place in a greased bowl, cover with a towel, and let stand for about 20 minutes. Refrigerate for 2 hours.

Remove from the refrigerator and place the dough on a lightly floured board. Roll it into a rectangle approximately 12 by 13 inches and about ½ inch thick. With a sharp knife or pizza cutter, cut the dough into twelve 1-inch-wide strips. For one cake, braid three of the strips into one rope. Repeat the process. Take both of the ropes and form one round rope. Repeat this braiding process for the second cake. Take the miniature

dolls and hide one in each cake, pressing them between the braids. (The person who finds the doll is King or Queen for the day.)

Place both cakes on ungreased cookie sheets. Cover with towels and allow to rise for about 45 minutes.

Preheat the oven to 400°F.

Beat the remaining egg and brush the cakes with it. Sprinkle the tops with the pecans. Place in the oven and bake for 20 minutes. Let cool.

To make the topping, mix with a wooden spoon the powdered sugar, vanilla, and enough water to form a thin paste in a small mixing bowl. Brush on the cakes after they have cooled. Now divide the sugar into three ⅓-cup portions in separate bowls. Add several drops of food coloring (green, yellow, and blue) to each portion and mix. Sprinkle this colored sugar in stripes on the cakes.

MAKES 2 CAKES

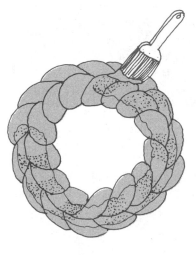

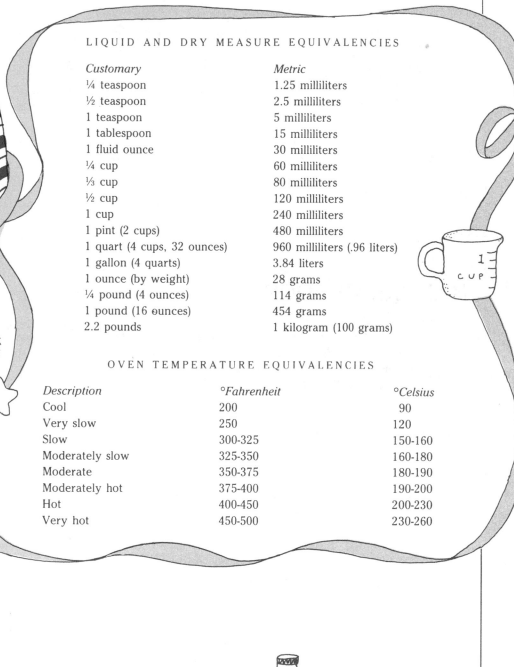

LIQUID AND DRY MEASURE EQUIVALENCIES

Customary	Metric
¼ teaspoon	1.25 milliliters
½ teaspoon	2.5 milliliters
1 teaspoon	5 milliliters
1 tablespoon	15 milliliters
1 fluid ounce	30 milliliters
¼ cup	60 milliliters
⅓ cup	80 milliliters
½ cup	120 milliliters
1 cup	240 milliliters
1 pint (2 cups)	480 milliliters
1 quart (4 cups, 32 ounces)	960 milliliters (.96 liters)
1 gallon (4 quarts)	3.84 liters
1 ounce (by weight)	28 grams
¼ pound (4 ounces)	114 grams
1 pound (16 ounces)	454 grams
2.2 pounds	1 kilogram (100 grams)

OVEN TEMPERATURE EQUIVALENCIES

Description	°Fahrenheit	°Celsius
Cool	200	90
Very slow	250	120
Slow	300-325	150-160
Moderately slow	325-350	160-180
Moderate	350-375	180-190
Moderately hot	375-400	190-200
Hot	400-450	200-230
Very hot	450-500	230-260

RESOURCES

CHRISTMAS BOOKS

The Christmas Sky, by Franklin M. Branley. New York: Thomas Y. Crowell Co., 1990.

The Twelve Days of Christmas, illustrated by Louise Brierley. New York: Henry Holt & Co., 1986.

Arthur's Christmas, by Marc Brown. Boston: Little, Brown & Co., 1984.

We Wish You a Merry Christmas: Songs of the Season for Young People, arranged by Dan Fox. New York: The Metropolitan Museum of Art, and Arcade Publishing, Inc., and Boston: Little, Brown & Co., 1989.

The Mole Family's Christmas, by Russell Hoban. New York: Scholastic, Inc., 1969.

The Family Read-Aloud Christmas Treasury, selected by Alice Low. Boston: Little, Brown & Co., 1989.

Merry Christmas, Festus and Mercury, by Sven Nordgvist. Minneapolis: Carolrhoda Books, Inc., 1989.

Carols for Christmas. Compiled and arranged by David Willcocks. New York: The Metropolitan Museum of Art and Henry Holt & Co., 1983.

HANUKKAH BOOKS

A Picture Book of Jewish Holidays, by David A. Adler. New York: Holiday House, 1981.

Jewish Days and Holidays, by Greer Fay Cashman. New York: SBS Publishing, Inc., 1979.

The Complete Book of Hanukkah, by Kinneret Chiel. N.J.: KTAV Publishing House, Inc., and Friendly House Publishers, 1959.

Treasures of Chanukah, illustrated by Greg Hildebrandt. N.J.: Unicorn Publishing House, 1987.

I Love Hanukkah, by Marilyn Hirsh. New York: Holiday House, 1984.

Potato Pancakes All Around: A Hanukkah Tale, by Marilyn Hirsh. Philadelphia: Jewish Publishing Society of America, 1982.

Hanukkah Pop-Up, by Sol Scharfstein. KTAV Publishing House, Inc., 1983.

Hanukkah! by Roni Schotter. Boston: Little, Brown & Co., 1990.

Chanukah A–Z, by Smadar Shir Sidi. New York: Adama Books, 1988.

The Power of Light: Eight Stories for Hanukkah, by Isaac Bashevis Singer. New York: Farrar-Strauss-Giroux, 1980.

Beni's First Chanukah, by Jane Breskin Zalben. New York: Henry Holt & Co., 1988.

Holiday cake pans and other baking and decorating paraphernalia can be ordered from: Wilton Enterprises, Inc., 2240 West 75th Street, Woodridge, Illinois 60517, or call (708) 963-7100. They have several catalogs that are priceless for finding any baking accessories. Some suggestions: a Christmas-tree cake pan ($7.99), a tree pan kit (2105-R-1510, $8.99), a mini Christmas tree pan (2105-R-1779, $7.99), cake-decorating sets (with tips included), and tips and instructions on decorating with icing.

CATFLIP by Jill Weber can be found at Penny Whistle™ Toys or write: FRAJIL FARMS, BOX 13, MONT VERNON, NH 03057

INDEX